CODENAME STALLION

BASED ON FIRST-HAND ENCOUNTERS WITH MILITANCY

ALOKE LAL IPS
MAANAS LAL

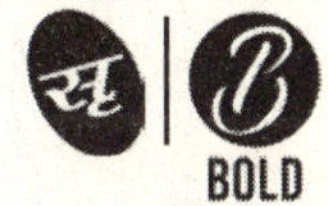

An imprint of
Srishti Publishers & Distributors

Srishti Publishers & Distributors
A unit of AJR Publishing LLP
212A, Peacock Lane
Shahpur Jat, New Delhi – 110 049

editorial@srishtipublishers.com

First published by Bold,
an imprint of Srishti Publishers & Distributors in 2024

10 9 8 7 6 5 4 3 2 1

This is a work of non-fiction, based on the authors' thorough research and experience. While due care has been taken to verify all information at press time, any inadvertent miss brought to notice shall be updated in the subsequent editions.

The book is partly based on the judgment of CBI special court, Allahabad High Court and police station records. Some elements in the story have been dramatized for the reader's pleasure. This narrative is not intended to in any way influence the ongoing legal process in the higher judiciary.

Printed and bound in India.

To the innocent victims of excesses by law enforcement agencies.

"Death is not the greatest loss in life. The greatest loss is what dies inside us while we live."

– Norman Cousins

Ballu

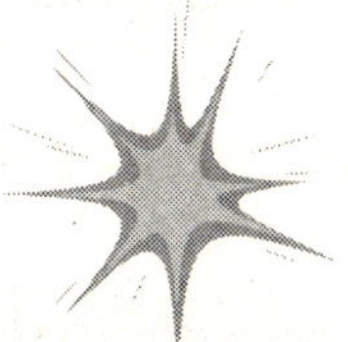

Just before sunrise, I scurried into the bylanes. I wanted to move fast but my feet felt heavy. The fog was thick and I was apprehensive of a potential collision with a passer-by. The lane that I had entered was becoming narrower. Above me, peeping through the dense fog was a complicated assortment of wires and cables. They looked like extensions of an invisible sky, a net that would keep me away from even a semblance of the divine.

My eyes fell on an elderly Sikh man with a sparse beard. It was as if the beard had been abraded by the winds of unpleasant experiences. He was illuminated by a street light that had been diffused by the fog. He was the perfect subject for a portrait of despair. I tapped on his shoulder but he did not respond. I tried again. He briefly lifted his sunken head to meet my eyes and then looked down again.

I asked him, "Sardarji, where is Balvinder Singh's house?"

There was no response. He continued to look down expressionlessly.

I had little time to waste and decided to take an even narrower lane to the left. This street was littered with festive décor. It looked as though a wedding had taken place the previous evening. Marigolds lined the road, but they looked ominously pale. The lane ended in a fork where I could spot another elderly Sikh man. He had features that were strikingly similar to the one I had earlier spoken to.

I walked up to him and asked, "Sardarji, where is Balvinder Singh's house?"

He looked me in the eye with absolute listlessness. It was as though his eyes were made of stone. I couldn't gather the courage to ask him again.

It was getting cold. I looked down the roads on either side of the fork and decided to take the one which was not so well-lit. It looked like the proverbial 'less taken' one and by corollary, richer in terms of the collection of intelligence.

There was a continuous buzz of crickets that had steadily overtaken the atmosphere. I wanted to cover my ears but that would have been tantamount to a death warrant. This lane was strange. It smelled like rotten flesh. I was thrown back momentarily to the dismembered bodies that I had seen at the site of a train derailment.

After walking for half a mile, I saw another Sikh man sprawled on a chair. As I approached him, I noticed that he, too, looked eerily similar to the ones I had run into earlier. If anything, his wrinkles seemed even more pronounced.

I asked, "Sardarji, where is Balvinder Singh's house?"

Finally, I got a response. The man pointed at the ground behind me. I could see a trail of blood, marked by my footsteps. My heart sank as I turned back towards the Sikh man. He was gone. The chair on which he was seated was gone too.

The drains on either side of the road had begun to overflow in red blood. My ammunition boots were soon soaked and I retraced my path as fast as I could.

As I crossed the lanes that I had previously mapped, I could not spot any of the sardars to whom I had spoken. The fog had lifted but there was no clarity in my thoughts.

My voice was ringing in my mind like an incessant morning alarm saying, "Sardarji, where is Balvinder Singh's house?"

***

This nightmare still revisits me, thirty-three years down the line.

***

Ostrich Politics

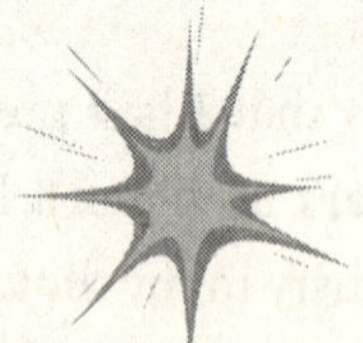

"What has been happening, Aloke? I had the impression that you have a bright future, but having heard about your performance as Superintendent of Pilibhit Police, I am sorely disappointed." This is what Trinath Mishra said to me at an election meeting which was being addressed by Prime Minister Chandra Shekhar in 1991.

Mishra was heading the Special Protection Group at the time, which was in charge of the prime minister's security. I was the officer looking after the PM's security at the meeting, which was a part of an ongoing election campaign. Chandra Shekhar's government had been dismissed following the withdrawal of support by the Rajiv Gandhi-led Congress party and the process of an election had been set in motion.

This was a troubled time in the history of the nation. There was a serious balance of payment crisis which was threatening to plunge the economy into depths from which a recovery would have been a great challenge. The Khalistan militancy had moved past its most troubled peak, though it was still alive in one way or the other. The government at the centre was propped up by support from outside by the Congress party. Thus, the Congress enjoyed an enviable position – that of being the king-maker with all the perks that only treasury benches could offer them, yet, have nothing to do when something went wrong and responsibilities were to be fixed.

In this sordid scenario, the nether side of political parties hardly presented a palatable picture. In many other countries, challenges of historic dimensions bring the most disparate political outfits together. The individual images of political actors cease to have larger than life proportions. For all the stakeholders, the presence of a potent enemy is the glue that brings them together to present a united and impregnable entity. But, alas, we do not seem to have that unifying force in India. While the financial crisis deepened, political parties continued to vie for petty victories among themselves.

On the allegation that two Haryana policemen were snooping on Rajiv Gandhi at the behest of the government, his party pulled the rug from under the cobbled-up government of Chandra Shekhar, forcing mid-term elections at a time when the country could ill afford the enormous expenditure that such an exercise entailed. The finance minister of those troubled times, Yashwant Sinha said, "It was not really a case of two Haryana policemen pushing the economy to the brink. The lesson I learnt was that in India, 'It's always politics, stupid!' 1991 is a lesson that, come what may, whatever be the depth of the crisis, we will not give up politics, (and) the nation be damned."[1] Thus, while the national government was struggling to remain afloat amidst all-time low political moves, the Mulayam Singh Yadav-led government in Uttar Pradesh was surviving precariously on ventilator support. It could barely afford any fresh problems coming its way. If they did, Yadav needed to face the issues arising from them.

One of the problems which had started to simmer in parts of Uttar Pradesh was the fallout of the ebbing Khalistan militancy in Punjab. As the movement weakened and the rank and file of the militant groups started to split, the groups became insecure with the police gaining the upper hand. Some of the militants moved out of Punjab to areas where they thought they were safe from the approaching police forces and could bank on the local Sikh population for shelter. The secure havens would also afford them the opportunity to think of renewed strategies and regrouping.

It became quite clear towards the latter part of 1990 that there was a presence of armed Sikhs in the Terai belt of Uttar Pradesh. There were Sikh families who had moved to this very inhospitable terrain at the time of the partition of the country in 1947. Over the decades, the hard-working Sikhs had cleared many jungles, fought off threats posed by wild animals as well as epidemics like malaria and had graduated to being prosperous farmers. While there was no evidence of militant tendencies among these Sikhs, the fact that the fleeing militants were looking for help was one that could not be overlooked. These militants were armed, had

---

1 Yashwant Sinha writes on 25 years of reforms: 1991, The Untold Story - The Hindu https://www.thehindu.com/opinion/op-ed/1991-the-untold-story/article14513325.ece

participated in violent action back in Punjab and were heroes to many. They were also not averse to using strong-arm tactics to find shelter, even when it was denied. They were also looking for money and food.

While the Sikh population has an inbuilt tendency to help all those in need, there were quite a few who doubted the intentions behind amassing money. The question that was troubling them was: why do these men need such huge amounts of cash? After a few weeks, the situation became clear. The money was required for arms and ammunition. There was also a need to raise groups of sympathisers among the local population. At this stage, the local intelligence units had become aware of the disturbing trends. The media was also mentioning the presence of unsettling undercurrents.

In its September 1990 issue, the widely read magazine '*India Today*' captioned one of its stories thus: PUNJAB TERRORISTS TARGET POLICEMEN IN UTTAR PRADESH. The story opened with these lines: "There is no containing the terrorists from Punjab who have gradually managed to convert the Terai region in northern Uttar Pradesh into a new base. Nearly two years after their movements came under the scrutiny of the state police, it seems that the terrorists have changed tack."

"If the earlier terrorist attacks were mostly on prosperous Sikh farmers based in the Terai (*India Today*, 31 May), two daring attacks on 4 September in Shahjahanpur and Pilibhit districts show that their strategy now is to primarily target policemen and informers."

The same news story went on to add: "It should have been clear to the police much before the terrorists struck in such a calculated manner. For over the last two years, the terrorists have killed twelve policemen in the region. Darshan Singh Ghora, a listed terrorist who was arrested in July in Punjab, had ambushed one SI and two constables in Pallai in October 1988. A senior official revealed that he had written to the government a dozen times. 'But nobody seems to be bothered,' he said."

The report also quoted the Deputy Inspector-General (DIG) Police of Nainital Range, S. M. Nasim, about his views on the militant activity in his jurisdiction: "They may want to create trouble here to pressure the government by spreading their activity outside Punjab."

The story concludes with a prophecy: "The terrorists have come and struck quite a few times, but the ill-equipped police with their .303 rifles are waiting for the government to help with equipment and money to mount an offensive. But there are no indications of any major operation being planned to save the beautiful Terai region from resounding forever with the rasping crackle of automatics."[2]

It was not long after the happenings of September 1990, that I was posted to Pilibhit as Superintendent of Police. My previous stint at Shahjahanpur had provided me with a fairly insightful background of the real happenings in the adjoining district of Pilibhit. Within weeks of taking over the reins of my new assignment, I authored a report to my superior officers and the government of Uttar Pradesh about the realities, as they existed

---

2 New tack - India Today https://www.indiatoday.in/magazine/indiascope/story/19900930-punjab-terrorists-target-policemen-in-uttar-pradesh-813071-1990-09-29#ssologin=1#source=magazine

on the ground. District Magistrate (DM) Sharda Prasad was the other officer to put his signature on that report. We were both of the view that the Sikh militants had grown in strength and that their resources had reached a stage where the ill-equipped Terai district police forces were proving to be far too short of requirements. Wealthy Sikhs were being forced to finance these activities. Women were not safe. They were being exploited by the armed militants and the local Sikh population had to face other humiliations as well. The attacks on those who were police informers were making our job tougher by the day. Our vehicles, arms and ammunition and communication equipment were falling short of even the most basic standards.

The DM and I knew that we could not keep waiting for the upgradation of facilities to meet the challenge before us. We evaluated our available resources. It was decided that there was a need to make our police stations and other offices safer. The security details were revised. The personal staff posted with senior officers was put under the scanner to ensure that there were no loose ends there. We also decided that we should have at least one car or any other vehicle in our possession which had no official markings or blue beacon lights. It was a conscious effort on our part to be careful about precautions while moving around. A part of this exercise was to have the drivers and gunners in plain clothes and even use false registration number plates on our cars. All this was done as part of a standard procedure which is followed across the world, wherever a militancy situation prevails.

It was with reference to all of this that Trinath Mishra thought I had proved to be a pansy by buckling under the militant threat. He told me that he had heard about the PM having spoken to the Chief Minister of Uttar Pradesh, regarding what he called 'cowardly' actions of the district officials of Pilibhit. The PM thought that the precautions we had taken were tantamount to the surrender of the whole administration before a handful of criminals. I explained our reasons to the senior cop and after a while, he supported what we had done and even tried to convince me that I should fill up one of the vacancies in his organisation, the Special Protection Group, at the SP-level.

Meanwhile, back in Lucknow, the capital of Uttar Pradesh, a hastily convened cabinet meeting of the government was in progress. The Chief Minister had summoned the Chief Secretary, Home Secretary and the Director-General of Police to the meeting. Mulayam Singh Yadav was livid, "Who has sent these immature kids to Pilibhit? They are saying that there are militants in the district. How foolish is that? Why will Sikhs leave Punjab to operate in the Terai of UP? They are bringing a bad name to the state." The senior minister, Beni Prasad Varma quipped, "Netaji (this is how Mulayam Singh Yadav was addressed by his associates), I know Aloke Lal. Many years ago he was the SP in my home district, Barabanki. He was known for his good work there, especially the crackdown on the opium mafia. What has happened to him now?"

"Yes, Varmaji, he was good at Shahjahanpur too. That is why we selected him for Pilibhit. But now look at him; he is talking about Sikh militants in Pilibhit! Listen DG *sahib*, I want a report from the Inspector-General (IG) of the Zone. The PM is furious that during this time of elections, we are talking about Sikh terrorism in UP. We must take these officers to task."

The DGP asked A. P. Mishra, the IG of Bareilly zone, to send a report immediately. Mishra, a wisened officer of long standing, understood the nature of report that would be best appreciated by the CM. He mentioned that there was no sign of militant activities; the district administration had misread the signals. Compare this to what he had told '*India Today*' only weeks earlier: "The recent cases were aimed to create terror. These were not just survival crimes which the terrorists have been committing in the past in this region."[3]

It should have been noted by Mishra that the media had reported a large number of violent acts of the militants in the year 1990, some of which are:

On 6 February, a bomb explosion in the crowded Laxmi Talkies of Haldwani, led to the killing of six and injuring of sixty-four persons.

A few weeks later, on 13 April, armed terrorists raided a farmhouse in Richaura village and killed the owner, Puran Singh and his wife. The terrorists left behind a note alleging that the couple had been killed because they were police informers.

On 17 April, the *jhala* (farmhouse) of Kashmir Singh in Bilsanda was attacked. He fired back but one of his men, Balkar Singh, fell to the terrorists' bullets.

On 22 April, Ajaayab Singh was shot dead.

---

3 Terrorism's new threat - India Today https://www.indiatoday.in/magazine/special-report/story/19900531-punjab-terrorists-establish-terai-as-their-new-base-812651-1990-05-30

S.P. Srivastava[4], the then Superintendent of Police, said, "In all these cases, the police recovered AK-47[5] shells from the spot. We have registered all four cases under the Anti-Terrorists Act and identified the gangs behind these killings." Apart from Pilibhit, there were cases of militant attacks in other parts of the Terai area as well.

On 12 March, three people on a motorcycle shot dead a constable who stopped them on the Haldwani-Rudrapur road.

One of the three assailants was the wanted terrorist Resham Singh, with a reward of twenty-five thousand rupees on his head. He had been living in Beria village since October 1988, running a clinic under the name of Dr Veer Singh. A search of the clinic revealed an exit hidden beneath the stretcher on which the fake doctor used to examine patients.

On 25 March, there was a bomb blast in a cinema in Kashipur, killing eight people and injuring twelve. The police suspected that the Resham Singh gang was behind the blasts.

In yet another sensational case, terrorists looted seventy-five thousand rupees from a bank in Kashipur.

Yet, the Inspector-General did not flinch from reporting just the opposite conclusion when he submitted his findings to the

---

4 Srivastava, my predecessor, was an effective leader of the district police force. His knowledge of both the terrain and the militants was excellent and it was largely due to his enterprise and leadership skills that Pilibhit was relatively in better control than some of the other affected districts. I have no hesitation in saying that the decision of the government to replace him at a crucial juncture in the operations against militants was a major contributing factor in what followed.

5 The Avtomat Kalashnikov is a sophisticated gas-operated assault rifle.

government. It was largely due to his watered down assessment of the gravity of the matter that what was perceived by the CM received confirmation – the DM and SP had gone too far when they sounded an alarm about the perpetrations of the militants. He surmised that it should be taken as an exhibition of their lack of experience. The government had indeed brushed facts under the carpet and the IG tasked with leading the charge against the militants in the area had played his role in this deceit that should have been avoided. Not surprisingly, both the DM and I were transferred. I was in that district for merely seven weeks.

My successor had the unenviable task of mounting his action from ground zero and reaching a benchmark that could be considered a vantage position. In operations against well-entrenched criminals, the task to work out a strategy based on a reliable knowledge of the terrain and the *dramatis personae* on the other side of the curtain is of vital importance. Given the pressure to deliver quick results, his task was fraught with moves which later analyses would denounce in no uncertain terms.

Was the government floundering at a time when firm handling based on foresight and understanding was the need of the hour? This is a question that will crop up whenever the matter of dealing with Sikh militants in Uttar Pradesh in the 1990s comes up.

* * *

Shahjahanpur

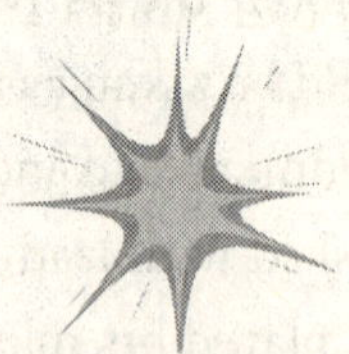

The district of Shahjahanpur has a rich and diverse history. Located about one hundred and seventy kilometres north-west of the state capital, Lucknow, on the highway leading to Delhi, Shahjahanpur has its name etched in the glorious history of India's freedom struggle. It was established by Dilir Khan and Bahadur Khan, sons of Dariya Khan, a soldier in the army of the Mughal emperor, Jahangir. Dariya Khan was originally from Kandahar in modern-day Afghanistan. Both Dilir Khan and Bahadur Khan were dignitaries during the regime of Shah Jahan. Pleased with the undying loyalty of Dilir Khan, Shah Jahan gave him seventeen villages in 1647, following the suppression of the rebellious Katheria Rajputs.

The immortal freedom fighters, Ram Prasad Bismil and Ashfaqulla Khan, were born in Shahjahanpur. Along with Chandrashekhar Azad, Rajendra Lahiri and a number of other accused, they were tried for conducting an alleged robbery of government funds near the Kakori railway station, on 9 August 1925. This case is famous as the 'Kakori Conspiracy'. Both Bismil and Ashfaqulla were hanged in 1927.

It is not merely violence and valour for which Shahjahanpur is known. The famous musical *gharana* which gave great sarod players like Enayat Ali, Ustad Murad Ali Khan, Ustad Mohammed Ameer Khan, Pandit Radhika Mohan Moitra and Pandit Buddhadev Das Gupta, also belongs to Shahjahanpur. The sarod maestro Amjad Ali Khan comes from the same gharana.

Shahjahanpur district has three rivers flowing through it – Ramganga, Gomti and Garrah. Kathana, Jhukma and Mensi rivers are tributaries of Gomti. Khannaut, Suketa and Kai rivers flow into Garrah. This results in rich, fertile agricultural land. Crops of wheat, millet, rice, maize, *bajra, jowar* and a number of lentils are commonly grown in this district.

The much talked-about Operation Blue Star in 1984[6] started a chain of uncontrollable events, which were classified under the broad umbrella of Sikh militancy. The assassination of Indira Gandhi was a direct outcome of this wave of militancy that had swept across several sections of North India. My first brush with

---

6 The codename 'Operation Blue Star' was given to a military operation carried out by the Indian security forces between June 01 and 10, 1984. The objective was to eject occupants led by Jarnail Singh Bhindranwale from the Golden Temple, the holiest site for Sikhs, which is located in Amritsar, Punjab. The decision to launch the operation was taken by the then Prime Minister of India, Indira Gandhi. It may be recalled that the state of Punjab had been gripped by prolonged militancy arising out of the demand to create a separate homeland, Khalistan, for Sikhs and was a major challenge for the governments at the centre and in the state. The action of the armed forces led to widespread resentment among the supporters of the demand. The Prime Minister, Indira Gandhi, was assassinated on 31 October 1984. Many parts of the country erupted into retaliatory violence unleashed on the Sikh community and businesses.

the movement for Khalistan was in 1989 when I was posted in Shahjahanpur. The movement for Khalistan, a separate homeland for the Sikhs, had petered out and split into factions by that time. There were some reports of suspected militant activities in and around Shahjahanpur but nothing concrete ever came of these leads.

The Powayan sub-division is in the northern part of the district. The Powayan, Khutar and Banda police station jurisdictions have Sikh populations and this area shares borders with the Terai districts of Pilibhit and Lakhimpur Kheri, which have many areas of sizeable Sikh presence. It was in these pockets of Sikh population that the movement of armed Sikhs of doubtful antecedents was noticed. When intelligence of this nature is collected at the ground level, it is necessary to accept that a problem is brewing and that there is a need to mount a suitable response from all concerned. In most cases, however, the tendency is to hush up what is simmering and allow matters to come to a boil and reach much larger proportions. The response of some of the senior officers was along these expected lines of denial. To exacerbate matters, the complete denial of the then state government to accept the presence of terrorists within their borders did not help.

Shahjahanpur was notoriously criminal, even by Uttar Pradesh standards. Murders were par for the course and there was hardly a day when we were not engulfed by several intricate investigations. I distinctly remember one case in which three members of a joint family ended up killing each other over a minor land dispute that arose from a small, perhaps unintentional, deviation in the angle of a boundary wall. Cases of minor disputes leading to serious violence of the nature seen in this case of the Tilhar area, were frequently reported. The propensity of being criminal was the primary reason why such incidents were considered to be just flashes in an already seething pan. In those days, forensic evidence was hard to gather and any analysis of such evidence ran into weeks, the kind of time in which most murder trails went cold. As a result, the police were always in the field, hunting for what is considered 'clinching' evidence in legal terms. My complete absence on the personal front was something that my family had come to expect in those days. Whenever I failed to make it in time for dinner, it was presumed that I was following one murder trail or the other.

Shahjahanpur was also a particularly arduous time for my wife, Madhu, who had to contend with one emotional challenge after another. The first and perhaps the most potent one, was the irreparable setback of losing her father, barely three weeks after his retirement from service as a medical professional. Unfortunately, his last days were spent chasing clerks to get his rightful pension sanctioned, something which should never have been the case for a person who retired as the chief of his service. Adding to this time of severe emotional strife was a desolate campus in Shahjahanpur, acres of farmland with only the occasional farmhand with whom to interact. A virtually absent husband chasing after murderers could not have been easy to contend with either. A solitary *mazar* in a corner of the enormous campus was her only place of prayer and refuge. Shahjahanpur, however, has a very special place in our hearts. It was here that our son Maanas came into our lives. This was cause for a much-needed cheer.

While in Shahjahanpur, I ensured that the police force came down heavily on the jungle mafia which was engaged in large-scale felling of trees. In fact, action was taken against some men in uniform who were seen to be hand in glove with the jungle mafia in the unsanctioned chopping down of trees. It was for this zeal as an environmentalist that I was hand-picked by Maneka Gandhi during her first term as Member of Parliament, to be the chief of police in her constituency of Pilibhit. It might appear unusual that the choice of the police chief of a district would be made on the basis of the credentials of an environmental conservationist, but Maneka Gandhi is known for her passion for wildlife and forest conservation. Pilibhit continues to be a political stronghold for Maneka Gandhi, the baton of which has been passed on to her son, Varun.

It may be recalled that in September 1990, Sikh militants attacked a police informer Kashmira Singh, 80, injured him seriously, killed his son Surinder Singh, 45, as well as three other people and injured fourteen others, who were travelling in a bus from Puranpur in Pilibhit to Bilsanda via Banda in Shahjahanpur. According to the media, two Sikhs with sling bags containing AK-47 rifles, boarded the bus at Banda. Soon after the bus started moving, they pointed their rifles and fired indiscriminately at Kashmira and his son.

A probe revealed that the next shootout after three hours in the adjoining district of Pilibhit, was a follow-up of the first shooting. The SHO of the police station at Bilsanda (Pilibhit district), Bachan Singh, decided to alert Kashmira's relatives, Tota Singh and Vir Singh, who lived in a farmhouse near Collectorganj village, three kilometres from the Bilsanda police station. According to *India Today*, Bachan Singh "took ten constables armed with just six SLRs, three .303 mm rifles and one .12 bore gun. When the police team was just half a km away from Tota Singh's farm at around 10.30 p.m., it was ambushed. The exchange of fire continued till 1.30 a.m."[7]

The Superintendent of police of Pilibhit, S.P. Srivastava and I, met at the border of our districts and after making an assessment of the seriousness of the situation, decided to meet our senior officers, the DIG and IG in Bareilly. The DIG was out of station; therefore, we met the IG. He agreed with our assessment that from the tenor of the incident, the violence involved and the use of sophisticated AK-47 rifles, as told by eyewitnesses, it was correct to conclude that militants had well and truly announced their presence on the soil of Uttar Pradesh.

***

While I was on my way back to Shahjahanpur from the meeting at Bareilly, I decided to take a detour. I wanted to obtain a first-hand idea about the section of the road linking Puranpur and Bilsanda in Pilibhit that passed through the police station in the Banda area in Shahjahanpur, so as to plan police readiness for any recurrence of the September 1990 incident. I sent a radio signal to the SHO Banda to be at hand on the road while I passed through the area under his jurisdiction.

---

7 New tack - India Today https://www.indiatoday.in/magazine/indiascope/story/19900930-punjab-terrorists-target-policemen-in-uttar-pradesh-813071-1990-09-29#ssologin=1#source=magazine

When I reached the spot after driving for almost an hour, dusk had set in. I met Shrikant Mishra, the SHO, on the road. We discussed all possibilities. I decided to walk some distance into the thicket growing by the roadside. I wanted to see what the possibilities of laying ambushes were should we need to intercept vehicles. As I stepped in, I immediately fell into a ditch which I could not see due to the foliage and failing evening light. Mishra, who had stepped in immediately after I had, also fell into the ditch and landed on top of me. His whole weight was borne by my right leg as his foot landed halfway between the knee and ankle. I felt an excruciating pain and for a moment, I thought that my fibula had fractured. As I moved a little and looked up, I found that Mishra had regained his composure before I had. He had wisely carried a flashlight with him and had the presence of mind to pull it out to assess the situation. He looked at my state and started to apologise immediately for having fallen on top of me. I knew that it was not his mistake at all, but when I told him that he was not at fault, he started to thank me for my 'large-heartedness'!

Mishra helped me climb out of the ditch and continued to curse himself throughout for what had happened. Once out of the ditch, I tried to stand but the pain was too much for me to put any weight on my left leg. It was courtesy Mishra and my driver that I could, somehow, reach my car and sit down. By then, the blood was oozing out from a wound below the left knee. The trousers were sticking to my skin and with some difficulty I pulled them up enough to see a gaping wound. I had a handkerchief, with which I made a futile effort to stop the flow of blood.

The attention was on me all this while. Mishra's injuries were being completely ignored. Due to my pain, I forgot to check with him as well. All the fuss was about my injury. The fact is that this was only to be expected. How often does it happen that when there are injuries, it is always the senior officer who receives all the attention and the junior one is ignored? Mishra was attending to my discomfort and pain but did not mention even once, the injury he had sustained on his thigh was bleeding. It seems as though there is a hierarchy of injuries too, based on who has suffered them.

Mishra offered to escort me to a hospital but I declined his gallant offer. I told him to go to the nearest facility and get himself treated.

When I returned to the district HQ, I was surprised that a couple of officers were waiting for me at the city outpost. They piloted my car straight to the district hospital. At the hospital, there appeared to be a buzz that I had been injured and senior doctors were waiting to attend to me. The next surprise was that they took me straight to the operation theatre. I thought that the injury in question could have been treated as an ordinary occurrence but the way in which they were handling me, indicated that the information that SHO Shrikant Mishra had passed on, made the matter appear to be far more serious than I thought it was. The doctors asked me many questions about where I felt pain, how had the injury occurred and some other similar questions.

I had my first taste of being the centre of attention of not one, but three doctors and a couple of nurses. With a few lights focused on my body from above, a thorough examination was carried out. They made me move my limbs and to my relief, after a few more observations, they concluded that there was no fracture and that the gash which was bleeding profusely had not ruptured deep enough to cause any serious damage. They cleaned the wound meticulously and dressed it. They advised me bed rest and minimum movement for at least three to four days. They warned me that it would be foolhardy to take the wound lightly and the possibility of septic or other infections was not ruled out. "Vigorous movements come with the danger of the resumption of bleeding," I was told by the senior doctor in the team.

I returned home to find a worried wife. Apparently, the news which she had received was alarming and it was a matter of great relief for her to find that her worst fears had proved to be unfounded.

I took a painkiller and a sleeping pill. My comfort level during the night was not such that I could get sufficient rest. As I got out of bed, I was told that the Circle Officer (Deputy Superintendent of Police) of the Powayan circle had made frantic efforts to contact me a number of times early in the morning.

The Sikh population of the district was concentrated in the Powayan circle. The militants' issue was uppermost in my thoughts since the previous evening. Therefore, it was something that I could not have taken lightly. In a matter of minutes, I put a call through to the circle officer, Madhukar Singh.

"Madhukar, tell me what is it that you wanted to speak to me about?"

"Sir, it is important. But I understand that you are injured, so I do not want to disturb you. I have been in touch with the additional

SP. Sir, I will seek his guidance. You please take rest."

"Rest? How is it possible? When I know you have something important to convey, how do you think I will have the peace of mind to rest? Tell me, what is important?"

"Sir, I have received definite information about the presence of Mark Stallion[8] in a village close to the Khutar police station. He is said to be with three other unidentified men who are carrying weapons which appear to be AK-47 or other sophisticated ones. They do not stay at one place together and their stay at the homes of local residents is short, at the most for two hours. They seem to have identified their hosts carefully. All of them are locals who might be sympathetic to the K-cause."[9]

"What is the force available apart from the *thana* staff?"

"Sir, we have half a platoon (about fifteen men) of the Provincial Armed Constabulary (PAC) armed with SLRs."[10]

"Okay Madhukar, organize the force close to the villages where you feel such a move can be made without attracting undue attention. I am dispatching a platoon of the PAC from nearby areas to augment firepower. We may have to go for an all-out offensive. Keep E-battery[11] ready. Ask the force to wear bulletproof vests and heavy steel helmets. There should be no laxity in this. I am making a move within minutes and should reach you in an

---

8 Code name for a dreaded militant who was reported to be hiding in Terai on being pursued vigorously by the Punjab police.

9 The Khalistan cause.

10 Self-loading Rifles.

11 Our code for keeping the option of an armed encounter in mind and following SOP.

hour. Let's show the bastards what the UP police is capable of."

"Sir, are you sure you can come? Can you move about, crawl and run in chase?"

"I am becoming better thinking about what we might be doing a little later. I have forgotten all my pain. Now, do as I have told you. We have no time to waste."

"Sir, well, I mean, are you sure... Additional SP sir is already on his way. He can guide us."

"Now, please don't bother about me and stop telling me what I should do. Don't waste time; it is the most precious resource in such situations. Keep your informants at hand. They should not be let out of sight even for a few minutes."

As I wore my uniform, I realized that I needed to swallow a couple of painkillers before I could make a move. I suspected that it would be a while before the pain would subside but the drive to get into action was such that after a while, I stopped thinking about it. As I made a move to leave home, my wife stopped me.

"Where are you off to?"

"I have an important meeting."

"Meeting...? An important meeting? Forget about it. You are not going anywhere." There was absolute authority in the manner in which these words were spoken.

I knew that I could not have left without convincing her that my presence at the 'meeting' was essential and there was no way in which I could have avoided it.

"I will be gone for only about an hour, Madhu. By the time you are through with your and Maanas's bath, I'll be back," I lied.

"It is not a matter of time; it is your injury. You may aggravate it. No, understand it loud and clear – you are not going anywhere, you are staying at home!"

Just as she dismissed any plans I had to attend the 'meeting', the radio telephone walkie-talkie set lying close by announced, "SP sir from CO Powayan."

I lunged for the wireless set and said, "Carry on CO Powayan."

"Sir, Mark Stallion stayed in the village Ranmastpur last night and is reported to have moved towards Lalpur Azadpur. My source is confident about the information that he may target a bank in Daulatpur tomorrow. What are the instructions, sir?"

I was in a quandary. On the one hand, I had an urgent call of duty and on the other, my wife was telling me to take care of myself. I was driven by the urge to answer the former, even though she had come up with irrefutable wisdom. I was wondering whether this was the time to bring some drama into the conversation and make an emotional pitch, by putting across a quote from some famous poem by Tennyson, extolling the virtues of duty before self. The well-known lines, 'Theirs not to make reply, theirs not to reason why, theirs but to do and die' sprang to my mind. I rejected this thought quickly, knowing that hyperbole never worked with my life partner.

While this conundrum was keeping me in a fix, the wireless set once again blurted out a message at just the wrong time, "SP sir from CO Powayan."

"Carry on."

"Sir, we are now in good numbers. We will make a move after your briefing."

"Okay, I'll be there with you as soon as possible."

All this was said within earshot of someone who I thought would now dig her heels in deeper. She would have surely understood what kind of 'meeting' it was that I had mentioned to her. As I turned to look at her, I found a changed expression.

"So, you were telling me that there is a 'meeting' to avoid mentioning the real thing. I know that you are required to lead the troops into a serious exchange. I can understand that there could be a showdown in which an exchange of fire cannot be ruled out."

After a short pause, she continued, "Aloke, you are in no physical condition to walk, let alone run, especially when you have a weapon to carry with you. It is difficult for me to imagine how you will endure this rigour. Yet, it is a delicate matter. In a situation like this, it will be wrong not to lead the men from the front." She paused again and added, holding back tears, "Go... be there."

I picked up little Maanas in my lap and hugged him before I left. He was just a little over a month old. He was not aware of the danger into which I was likely to walk.

As I sat in the car, I winced with pain. I was carrying painkillers with me and decided that on reaching the scene of action, I would take two more of them.

On the way, I thought many times about what Madhu had said to me. The message was – I must lead from the front.

Net Practice

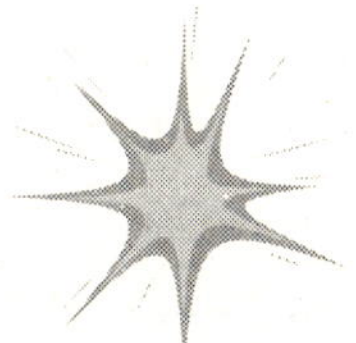

The road to Powayan was mostly good and the progress was satisfactory. There were some poorly maintained stretches too, which posed a challenge to an injured traveller due to the jumps and jerks. On reaching the destination, when I saw my men eagerly waiting for my instructions to get on with the action, I forgot all my pain. The concern for making the plans clear down to the last man in the rank and file was uppermost in my mind. I was also aware that I needed to appear not only in a state of top battle worthiness, but also, exude the confidence that triumph was going to be ours that day.

The first stage of the briefing was to gather knowledge about the available intelligence at the police station level. The important aspect of knowing the contours of the terrain was next. The presence of water bodies including canals was a concern because the monsoon had been generous that year and we had many water-inundated areas in the terrain where the action was to take place. We needed to know the vegetation for planning our camouflage. The likelihood of wildlife, especially reptiles, leeches and scorpions which were common there, was another factor to be kept in mind. Bridges, culverts, state of the roads and the attitude of the local population were some of the other points for discussion. We needed to know with a certain degree of assurance who we could consider as friends and what were the likely threats from those who might have reasons for nursing soft feelings for the ones who we considered to be marauders. We also needed to keep in mind that in case of an encounter where guns would go ablaze, were we likely to cause collateral damage to the local populace? These are routine aspects of planning an encounter with violent lawbreakers, so it becomes like a checklist that gets created in an experienced cop's mind. The disregard for any boxes on this list, however insignificant they may seem, is many times the reason for failure.

The weapons we were likely to confront from the opposite side were an important factor to be taken into account. Madhukar Singh's information was that the dreaded AK-47 was likely to be the most formidable killing machine for which we needed to brace ourselves. As a special provision in the areas where the movement of militants was noticed, a few AK rifles were provided to the police stations. As a result, we decided that we should carry the four AK rifles that were available in the nearby stations during the operation.

My briefing of the officers and men detailed all that I thought was important. I answered questions. I made it quite clear that we were planning to confront the enemy a little before sunset. The possibility of darkness descending while we were in the chase made it necessary that no one should light a matchstick or cigarette lighter. Even talking was prohibited.

I asked the final question, "Are you ready, boys? Are there any doubts?"

I was answered with a resounding confirmation that the men were all set to pounce on the adversary.

As we ran, walked, jumped and crawled in the direction of our target, we went through a few experiences which appear trivial on the outside, but have serious implications for those in the thick of battle.

We were barely a quarter of a kilometre away from camp when we encountered a small but sobering experience. It was a leech with which we were to come face to face, if that could be an apt description of what happens when a leech finds its way into the heavy boot of a man and starts sucking blood. For a *jawan* freshly out of training school at the district headquarters, it came as a big shock to feel something foreign find its way through his socks and even the heavy shoe he was wearing. However, for the inch-long black little predator, it was routine to coolly start an operation it was only too adept at carrying out – that of feeding on human blood with a sucker at both the anterior (front) and posterior (back) ends. The *jawan* noticed this black muscular and relatively solid segmented abomination having established a camp on the calf muscle of his left leg, a sight which he was familiar with, only because he had seen pictures of leeches in some article carried by a newspaper. The very same article had given a rather exaggerated account of the damage that leeches could cause to the host body and, as often happens, the young *jawan* imagined that the worst was in store for him as well.

The worst fears of the *jawan* were immediately translated into a panic attack. Not only did he start wailing as if his dear life was on the hook, he also ran out of the bushes in which an entire section was lying in wait for a command for dealing with the militants. He had given away the location of a number of his fellow policemen who were sanguine in the belief that they were well-camouflaged. Clearly, this was a serious lapse and could not be taken lightly. He was pulled back rudely into the thicket by the section commander and received what must have been a painful whack on his ear. The leech was also suitably dealt with and normalcy was restored in the area of the commotion.

The *havaldar* lying in ambush next to me whispered in my ear, 'Sir, two o'clock, twenty-five metres, there's smoke." This was to convey to me that there was some smoke rising at about sixty degrees to the right of the straight line of vision. Yes, indeed, there was smoke and it was a giveaway in a battlefield. I asked the *havaldar* to crawl to the point from where the smoke was emanating and immediately have the nonsense stopped. It turned out that a sub-inspector could not control the urge to have a puff or two. He was a youngster who was participating in a tense encounter-prone situation for the first time. The newcomer was upbraided in stern words, with a handsome sprinkling of the unprintable, which I reckoned would stay with him for the rest of his life!

As the dusk brought down the visibility to just a faint shimmer, the auditory sense now dominated over the sense of vision. Every little sound could be heard in the silence that was being maintained by everyone in our party. In this calm stillness, a jarring metallic sound was disturbing me. I suspected that some irresponsible member of our party was creating the sound which, in the given circumstances, could make all the difference. After a while, we could make out from where the sound originated. It was a *jawan* who was feeling unsure if his rifle would cock at the crucial time and was, therefore, fiddling with the bolt. While this behaviour of the *jawan* underlined the general unpreparedness of police officials for battlefield conditions, it was also a commentary on the outdated machinery that the policemen have to depend upon in these situations, where the borderline between life and death is so tenuous. The cumbersome Lee-Enfield rifle continues to be the most common weapon with most of the police forces of the country, although it has been condemned by the armed forces several decades ago.

While the confidence of the *jawan* dealing with his insecurity about his weapon was being restored by his seniors, we heard a desperate, yet, suppressed whimpering from a few metres away. This time we found that a comrade was in a real pickle. He had stepped into a marsh and the fine clay beneath had made him virtually immobile. The more he tried to disengage himself, the more the hold of the soil around his feet seemed to gain in strength. Experienced trekkers know about such situations; so do soldiers who are called upon to negotiate marshy grounds. The situation was resolved by his fellow *jawans*. This experience also alerted all the others to the danger in which anyone amongst them could land.

The trickiest situation was the loss of composure of an officer. Somehow, he recalled that his young wife and three-month-old daughter were entirely dependent on him and his old, ailing father was to be continuously monitored for his blood pressure and blood sugar levels. This monitoring was done by him and in his absence, the values of these vital parameters were bound to be neglected. He started to sob all of a sudden and the entire team under him felt as if their leader was developing a level of nervousness that would make him a sitting duck. I crawled to the point where this drama was in progress.

I found that it was Sub-Inspector Heeralal Yadav with a visibly eroded morale and that surprised me. I had always thought of him as a promising youngster who could be an asset for the force one day. Here he was, all broken up. I kept a reassuring hand on his shoulder and asked him in whispers why he was so distraught. He shared his concerns about his family and suddenly, his sobbing acquired a much higher octave. I had to virtually gag him with my hand to control the noise that he was making. I spoke softly to him to explain how each member of our team shouldered different levels of personal responsibilities. Some were even more stressed than he was, yet when it came to duty, each one of us managed to keep our composure and focus on the job at hand. I told him that when we return from this operation, I would personally see to it that his father got the best possible treatment. He was placated appreciably when I heard one of our leading sections on my radio set signalling a south-eastern move for us as there was information of militant movement in a hamlet barely a stone's throw away. Heeralal Yadav assured me that he was completely in the frame of mind to continue our march in dealing with the militants we were pursuing.

All these happenings that take place in the thick of action are like a mirror to reflect on our readiness to deal with challenging developments. Our armaments, individual battle-worthiness, the management of the social life of our *jawans* and officers – all need to be seriously addressed. We have to abandon the tendency to forget in times of peace, what war time is like.

* * *

The highly dependable intelligence that Madhukar received at this precise time was about the location of the gang. The expression of his excitement was a spectacle. He must have expended a significant number of calories to quickly crawl close to me to whisper what he had learnt. The number of desperados was said to be about half a dozen and they were reportedly armed with at least two AKs. Their location was a *jhala* in village Tharbanpur Grant, located on NH730, in the jurisdiction of the police station in Khutar. We needed to make a move due SE (south-east) from where we were currently located. He assessed that the time required for us to encircle their hideout would be roughly an hour and we could immediately make our move.

The signal for a move due south-east was also the juncture at which we branched into three parties. The idea behind the split was to surround the militants on three sides and leave an opening on the fourth flank. Should they attempt an escape from the open side, we would be ready with an ambush party to deal with them on that route.

A little later, we heard from the other two parties. They had also reached their starting points and were asking for instructions to move in the direction of the *jhala* where the militants were said to be present. Our estimate was that we were likely to reach the location in about thirty minutes. The movement was to be made under cover and noiselessly.

Our estimate was nearly accurate and as expected, we were surrounding the *jhala* of Tejinder Singh. He was a dependable source about whom Madhukar had spoken in glowing terms. They had fixed a signal for exchanging the exact location of our parties and that of the gang. We were lying in wait for the signal to be exchanged when I felt that there was a movement very close to my right leg. I was tempted to use a torch to see what it was but it would have given away our location. It was certain that the gang must have created a post at a vantage point for someone to keep an eye all around for any suspicious movement.

At this very moment, a wireless message from Madhukar confirmed that our moment to strike had come. I gave him the go-ahead. It also gave me an opportunity to check what the movement was that I had felt only seconds earlier. A snake had found its meal, a mouse, and was in the process of enjoying it. I had no time to bother about this, so I warned the others in the party to be careful of the reptile when we moved. As per the pre-planned action, we started to move slowly closer to the *jhala*. When we were some twenty-five or thirty metres away from the target, Tejinder took the next pre-decided step – he informed the gang leader that he had noticed some movement around his *jhala*. The gang immediately took positions to face us and the person who was on watch at the top of a house, suddenly lost his balance and crashed to the ground. This was a fall of about twenty feet and he could not suppress a loud, agonizing scream. As he screamed, Madhukar's party opened fire from the west side. From the south side, we started to fire bursts, and the third party also did the same. This sudden onslaught seemed to rattle the gangsters and they retaliated by firing in our directions. It was at this stage that they must have decided to escape towards the open side in the north. It seemed as though they knew the area very well because they were able to cover a good distance very quickly. We were in pursuit, but knew that their speed was faster and the distance between us was increasing. I was not unduly perturbed because their movement was in the direction of the cut-off party, which had been alerted about the gang's movement and I was hopeful that we would be able to get them there. We continued to move in the direction of their escape. As we got closer to our cut-off party, we heard firing from their direction. For once, the sound of bullets made me happy. I was hopeful of success.

After about fifteen minutes, the firing died out. We reached closer to the scene of action and were able to exchange notes among ourselves. Three of our men had received minor bullet injuries and quite a few had hurt themselves while negotiating the uneven terrain. We also realized that we had lost the gang which took advantage of its superior knowledge of the terrain. A team was following the gang in the general direction in which it had escaped. The cut-off party was also in pursuit.

A little later, Madhukar's informer Tejinder joined us. Madhukar questioned him as to why the desperados were allowed to stay in the *jhala*. He said that they had no choice. Any resistance would have led to serious retributions. His whole family, including aged grandparents and children would have been exposed to danger.

We continued to gather more information from Tejinder and learned that the leader of this gang was Mark Stallion, one of the most hotly pursued militants. It was a case of being so near and yet so far! For me, there were lessons that I learnt in the conduct of raids by the police in the militancy-infested parts of the district.

The following morning, we had a debriefing session in which Madhukar told us that at least one of the gang members seemed to have received a bullet injury if the amount of blood loss was to be taken as an indication. This gave us hope that the combing operations in the area would bring us rewards.

I looked at it as net practice to prepare for the bigger game in which we were bound to engage at a later date.

***

Pilibhit

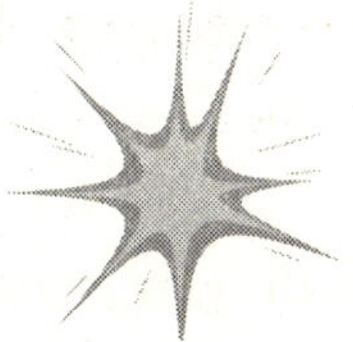

What connection do flute maestros like Pandit Hariprasad Chaurasia, Pannalal Ghosh and Ronu Majumdar have with the small town called Pilibhit, situated in the Terai area of Uttar Pradesh? The modest instrument made of bamboo with which these maestros and many others of their kind create magic in diverse parts of the globe is crafted in Pilibhit. This small town of just over one lakh people is famous for producing the best flutes in the world. In order to scale the levels that place the produced flute in the category the maestros prefer, the flute-maker must himself know how to play and be sensitive to *sur*, explains Khurshid Ahmed, whose family has been making flutes for four generations in a small workshop off the busy Lal Road. Ahmed claims that his ancestors made Lord Krishna's flute too.

The flute industry started to dwindle as the twentieth century drew to a close. The bamboo which was required for producing pro-level flutes came all the way from the forests of Silchar in Assam and the conversion of the railway line from the narrow to the broad gauge only till the nearby Bareilly meant that transportation of the bamboo became a long drawn out and costly process. Other factors also contributed to the severe slowing down of the tempo of mass-scale production of the instrument. It can be said that the early 1990s witnessed the replacement of the sonorous bamboo tubes called flutes by other tubes, which had nothing to do with soothing notes of music. The new tubes were another name for death: Kalashnikov rifles!

Pilibhit was in news in the year 1990, when tigers were sighted in its jungles bordering Lakhimpur district. There was active consideration to declare the area a tiger reserve after a couple of cubs were spotted moving about in the area adjacent to the Dudhwa National Park and the Nepal border.[12] In the early part of January that year, my wife Madhu and I took a short trip to a forest rest house in this area. I needed a break from my work in Shahjahanpur and there was a weekend which gave me the opportunity to plan the trip.

I left the guest house early in the morning in a jeep on being told that a male tiger had been spotted a couple of kilometres to the north of the guest house. Madhu rightly decided to stay back; she suspected that there could be bumps in the *kutcha* road. She was carrying Maanas as a five-month-old foetus.

As we drove off, I was hoping that I would have the great pleasure of seeing the lord of the jungle in its natural habitat.

---

12 Pilibhit Tiger Reserve, located in Pilibhit, Lakhimpur Kheri and Bahraich Districts of Uttar Pradesh was declared open in September 2008. It is India's forty-fifth Tiger Reserve Project. The northern edge of the reserve lies along the Indo-Nepal border while the southern boundary is marked by the river Sharada and Khakra.

I wanted to be one of those rare *Homo sapiens* who have the experience of seeing *Panthera tigris,* the magnificent big cat, in flesh and blood. Those who have seen this fabled embodiment of strength and ferocity up close without any hindrance are indeed, exceptionally lucky. I was hoping to be one of them as I drove through a jungle road with three others accompanying me, one of whom was the driver Krishna Singh, known for his intimate familiarity with the topography of those tracts. He also fuelled our hopes of seeing a tiger on this foray when he said that there was an unusual calmness around, which happened at times when the 'lord' was on his beat. He confirmed that tigers had been spotted in the recent past in the area where we were now looking for one.

We saw a number of deer, especially hog deer. The beauty and grace of these excellent sprinters was a wondrous sight to behold. Krishna thought aloud, "Are these deer so circumspect in their movement for avoiding noise which would attract a predator? Their silence and careful movements are a good omen." He signalled all of us to maintain silence and avoid smoking. He then stopped at a vantage point.

We lay in wait for almost an hour. We saw some other wildlife, mainly antelopes and a few primates too, but our sights were pining for something much more coveted. Krishna, our charioteer on this trip, said that the chances of realising our dream had receded as the animals around us were now engaged in business as usual. So, after spending a couple of hours on this wild goose chase (or shall we call it, a wild tiger chase), we decided to retrace our steps to the rest house. Throughout the drive, we were bemoaning our bad luck. Krishna was behaving as though it was his personal failure not to have made the trip a more memorable one.

Back at the rest house, there was a great deal of excitement. Madhu was grinning from ear to ear. Her glee was so profoundly writ across her face that her sight evaporated much of the gloom with which I was dealing. She asked me, "Tell me. How was the trip? Did you sight a tiger?"

"No. It was much ado about a squirrel! What is keeping you and all the others hyper here?"

"Has no one told you? I saw a tiger!"

"You saw a ...what? Don't tell me..."

"Yes, of course, a tiger!" She raised her voice to repeat, "A tiger!"

"How...where...? You must be joking."

"Right here. Yes, a tiger," she confirmed.

She told me that she had been sitting outside in the open lawn, enjoying the warmth of the sun. For a few minutes, complete stillness descended and even the birds seemed to have fallen silent. Then, she noticed some movement in the hedge at one end of the lawn. The next moment, a big tiger entered the lawn from that point. After entering, the monarch of the jungle surveyed the surroundings all around. It must have noticed her presence too. At that moment, her heart skipped not one, but possibly, a few beats. Then, the big cat resumed its walk across the lawn with all the feline grace for which it is famed. As it reached the other end of the compound, the tiger stopped again and took in the entire scene once more. It seemed to be satisfied with what it saw and then moved on, out of sight.

The *chowkidar* and the cook posted at the guest house told us that this was the first royal visit to their campus. The two were busy inside during the few minutes while the visit was underway and missed the spectacle.

I asked the sentry who was posted for security in view of our visit, "Where were you? Did you see the tiger?"

"I was at the gate on duty. I saw the tiger, sir. It was very handsome!"

"What did you do when you saw it? Did you take any action to deal with any dangerous situation which could have arisen?"

"Sir, I saw the tiger very close to its time of exit."

"What if it had decided to come back and attack somebody?"

"Sir, I was too mesmerised by the beauty of the beast. It did not occur to me that I needed to take position to shoot. I was hypnotised by the grandeur of the tiger."

Later, in the evening, as we were eating dinner, we revisited the day's happenings. We talked of the contrasting fortunes of one who went all the way to the jungle to see the king and that of the one who stayed back lounging in the sun, at whose abode, the king had come calling.

As we retired, I said to Madhu, "The tiger makes me yearn for more. Will I have the opportunity to serve in this district? Will we be able to bring our child here to see a tiger at close quarters?"

"As far as I am concerned, our child has already had the pleasure," Madhu responded.

* * *

My posting to Pilibhit district came in January 1991. The assumption of charge is a routine procedure but the undercurrent of expectations runs sharp. While the new incumbent has certain goals in mind, the officials who are already posted in the district have anxieties centred on the temperament of the new boss. They wonder about what priorities and value systems would govern his administration, would he be a hard taskmaster and would he have a hands-on style or allow freedom of action? In jobs that involve a tightrope walk, like the violence-prone police department in which the lives of the personnel are exposed to mortal danger, it is not uncommon to see the leader develop greater faith in the abilities of select individuals. Naturally, these individuals become a part of a shortlist of those who may be labelled as 'blue-eyed boys', leading to some degree of heartburn among the others. There is no denying the fact that key positions in the administration are also assigned to such preferred individuals. The turmoil of the favourites of the outgoing boss is most marked. As often happens, the incumbent boss is filled with all kinds of information that is not necessarily true by vested interests, to sway his opinions one way or the other. Coupled with this, is the inarguable fact that the boss is actually finding his way around in the new setting and making an effort to identify those members of the staff that have a track record which evokes the desired level of trust.

The official record of a police official's attributes is contained in what is commonly called the 'character roll'. There is a requirement that an annual confidential entry be made in it, giving an account of the work done over the year and a rating like 'excellent' (the best), 'very good', 'good' or 'poor' is also recorded. These entries are a good guide but can also be misleading if the reporting officer makes biased comments. This situation is, unfortunately, not uncommon. The individual likes and dislikes across the hierarchy are reflected in this record, making it difficult to make a fair assessment. This leaves the incumbent with a dilemma of whether to go by the record in the character rolls or to act on opinions that come thick and fast. Fortunately, there are a few officials whose performances are recorded with consistency by different assessing officers and can be taken as a dependable guide to judge their actual merits.

Luckily, I had complete faith in the judgment of my predecessor, S.P. Srivastava. I saw no need to make any changes. I decided that my innings was to be played with more or less the same team.

***

A 'Warm' Welcome

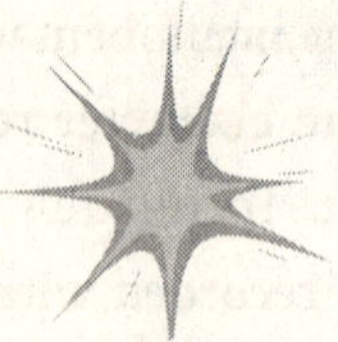

Winters in the Terai towns have a record of temperatures plummeting to near zero. The early morning sun on that Sunday in January was a great temptation to take a stroll in the compound. I thought that the welcome sunshine was the ideal setting to spend some precious time with Maanas, who was seven months old now. We had winged visitors, most notably parrots in large numbers, which caught the toddler's fancy and the delight on his face had the power to lighten my mood. While the pleasure of those strolls was precious, at the back of my mind was the fact that a few of my colleagues were waiting for me to hold an important discussion. So, Maanas had to be sent back into the house soon after.

The intended agenda of the meeting was to deliberate on our preparations to meet the challenge which was posed by the suspected presence of militants in the district headquarters. There was reliable intel that in the forest just outside the town, there was movement of some suspicious-looking men, their faces covered with the ends of the turbans and there being objects in their possession, whose outlines resembled those of weapons like Kalashnikov rifles. The sun was able to seduce me once again and I decided to hold our discussion in the open. I asked the other officers to come and join me for the meeting.

We were still in the process of being seated when I heard the inspector from my Local Intelligence Unit (LIU) say, “Sir, the threat appears to have spread to the outskirts of the town. Head Constable (HC) Balkar Singh is confident that the shadows he has noticed in the Mohof Range are not of local residents. Earlier, there was an input from the Eidgah area of about eight or nine suspicious characters being spotted on the banks of the Devha river. I would not rule out a possible strike at some sensitive location in the town itself.”

The circle officer (CO) in charge of the city interrupted, “Inspector sahib, your reaction is exaggerated. So far, we have no confirmation of any such movement.”

“Yes sir, we have been combing the outskirts for a week or more but have not intercepted anyone who could be suspected to be a militant,” was the assessment offered by the SHO of the Kotwali area.

I thought I needed to intervene as the two assessments presented were opposite to each other. “I must share with you the input from the Intelligence Bureau. They are of the view that the possibility of the presence of some militants cannot be ruled out. They also see a likelihood of a strike by them. Their agenda could include looting a bank or targeting some installation or person of consequence.”

The CO interposed, "Sir, these intelligence agencies..."

His voice trailed off as we noticed a man rushing towards us with great urgency. He jumped onto me, grabbing me with his outstretched hands. I fell down on the ground along with the chair on which I was sitting, with the intruder sprawled all over me. At this precise moment, there was a loud noise of gunfire. The sentry who was standing close to the gate opened fire in response. His shots alerted the other guards in the nearby guard room and they also came out, firing many shots with their weapons. This entire action was rapid and happened in a matter of a minute or two. The man who had jumped onto me, had in the meantime, stood up and composed himself enough to help me get back on my feet. I tried to recognise him but soon realized that I had never seen him before. He signalled me to crawl rather than walk. I could decipher that he was well-versed in battle moves. He gave me cover with his body so that I could move to the safety of the veranda where there was a wall and sand bags with the purpose of providing protection from gunshots.

A few minutes later, it was relatively quiet in the compound. The man who had played such a crucial role just minutes earlier, now advised me to move into my camp office room. I don't know how and what nature of spell he had cast on me that I was following his instructions without doubting his intentions. Once inside the office room, he greeted me with great respect. I looked at him quizzically. As if reading my thoughts, he introduced himself.

"Sir, I am Havaldar Roshan Singh of the CRPF. I belong to Bilsanda and am visiting my family these days. I have been granted long leave by my commandant on special grounds. I have come to pay my respects to you, sir."

"Havaldar, what happened outside? How was it that you suddenly pounced upon me?" I quizzed him.

"Sir, while entering your compound, I ran my eyes over the long boundary wall. I noticed three men sitting next to it. Their body language made me suspect their intentions. So, after I came inside, I continued to sit in a position from where I could keep an eye on the spot where they were sitting. You were interacting with the officers after sending the baby inside and I knew that a closer watch was needed to observe the move that I suspected could be made by those men."

"What happened then?"

"Sir, I noticed the appearance of the nozzle of a sophisticated weapon across the boundary wall. I thought that you could be the target and decided to take action. I am sorry to have made you fall on the ground, but I could think of no other way of protecting you."

"How did you conclude so quickly that I would be the target and not the other officers?"

"Sir, I guessed it. I thought that if they had taken the risk of raiding your residence, they were bound to have you as the target, not the others."

"You seemed to be right in your assumption because the shots passed very close to me, while the others were a few feet away."

"Sir, I had given my name and designation at the gate to be noted in the register kept for the purpose. I had a word with the sentry and told him about what I had observed. Having thus alerted him, I was sanguine that the guard room would rise to the occasion, if so needed. Luckily, they acted promptly when the attack took place."

I called the other officers inside, who were in the protected area of the veranda. I told the CO and SHO to immediately organize a thorough combing of the entire residential neighbourhood. They were told to take an armed company of the PAC from the police lines and carry out a door-to-door search in the areas that were adjacent to my compound and then fan out into the most prone areas of the town. I also told the SHO to make an entry in the records of the police station and prepare a draft FIR.

The officers swung into action immediately and barely twenty minutes later, messages were being exchanged in code language over the police wireless, confirmed the reassuring information that combing was underway. However, just outside the boundary wall, from the spot where the shooters had been seen earlier, nothing more than a couple of empty shells were recovered. It is surprising that the shooters had left behind tell-tale evidence of having used AK-47 rifles in the shootout – a sure indication that they were not ordinary criminals but militants possessing state-of-the-art weapons.

The LIU inspector asked me, "Sir, what are the instructions for me?" He pointed towards Havaldar Roshan Singh and added, "I am so glad that you were saved by this brave man." His attention shifted to the havaldar and he asked him who he was. The havaldar introduced himself. The intelligence officer wanted to be sure, so he looked at me once and then at him and said, "Please show me your ID card." The CRPF man seemed to be surprised that he was required to prove what he had said. He looked at me quizzically and I nodded to him to comply. He promptly took out a card from his pocket and the inspector examined it closely before returning it to him.

The inspector shuffled away.

I asked Roshan Singh to tell me the purpose of his visit to my camp office. He repeated that he was on special leave and that his family lived in Bilsanda, a township in the district.

"What is the meaning of special leave? I have not heard about it before," I asked him.

"Sir, I was with the Indian Peace Keeping Force (IPKF) deployed at Jaffna in Sri Lanka in the year 1988. Some of the happenings there greatly disturbed me. I witnessed the atrocities committed by our forces while the Tamil resistance was being crushed. I never thought that my fellow Indians could be so brutal. I was particularly disturbed by the reports of human rights violations by our soldiers there." He continued, "Women were raped. There were cases of sodomy, murder and torture. The reality that was all around me was more horrendous than anyone can imagine. I was disturbed and that is putting it mildly. In fact, I was shaken to my core."

I couldn't quite understand what had caused his personal anguish in the matter. Allegations of human rights violations by Indian troops deployed in Sri Lanka had been in the news for a few years. I wondered if the several thousand soldiers who were deployed for the peacekeeping task were affected in the same way as was Roshan Singh.

I asked him, "Roshan, the armed forces have a history of being at the receiving end of such allegations. Even if such happenings as you say had actually taken place, they could not lead to the emotional turmoil of the kind that you are exhibiting. There must be more to it, am I right?"

Roshan remained silent and there was angst writ large all over his face. Even his body language conveyed his torment. I thought that his silence spoke volumes, yet I was curious to dig into his personal tale.

I looked into his pained eyes and said, "Roshan..." I was at a loss for words and wondered how I should frame my query. I gathered the words that I thought would be appropriate and said, "Roshan, there is no need to open up on matters which you find to be too hurtful to narrate. I can understand that there is something which you are finding difficult to share. Don't worry. We will find other occasions to understand your distress." After a pause I added, "You can count me as a friend. Do not ever hesitate to ask me for any help you may need." I continued, "I have no means to pay you back for the great turn you have done me this morning. If it had not been for you, the story could have been so different. If I can do something for you, please do tell me."

He looked wide-eyed at me, tears welling up in his eyes. I noticed that he was on the verge of breaking down. His body was shaking. He seemed to be looking for something to hold, possibly, to stabilize himself. I offered him water and as he held the glass, some of the water spilled due to his shaking hands. I asked him to sit down. After a little hesitation, he sat down and drank some more water. He now looked reasonably composed to resume talking.

"Sir, I was a member of the CRPF group which was tasked with the work of clearing landmines which the Tamil militants had placed in the area where the army was to move for action. My buddy for this purpose was Venky..." His voice trailed off and I noticed that his lips were quivering. Once again, he appeared to be holding back tears. A couple of moments later he added, "I saw Venkat Narayanan blown to smithereens right in front of me as he accidentally stepped on a mine. In fact, Venky...," He trailed off again. He started to sob and took a little while to control himself before he resumed talking, "Pieces of Venky's flesh were strewn all around. I don't know what came over me... I ran from one spot to another, looking for pieces of him. I was picking up whichever piece of flesh I thought belonged to his now severely mangled body. I was drenched in his blood. My face was the colour of his blood." Roshan's body was rocking and he started to wail.

I went around the table and put a consoling hand on his shoulder. He continued to wail for a while and then, gradually composed himself.

He spoke haltingly between sobs, "Sir, I was completely broken by this loss. Venky and I were like brothers after having served in those conditions where violent barbarism was all around us. We found solace in each other's company. He talked about his village in Andhra Pradesh. He often told me about his two children. He sang Telugu songs. I had no idea what the words meant but enjoyed his sonorous renditions. His violent end and the manner in which it happened made me disconsolate. I began to feel that my life was futile. Somehow I believed that I was responsible for his end. I could not absolve myself of the responsibility."

"But there was no fault from your side. You were with him on the same duty. The explosion could have killed you as well. Why do you feel guilty of something you did not do?" I asked.

"Sir, I thought that I should have been there in his place. I thought about his family. I was still unmarried then and thought that my demise would have been a loss for fewer people. No one was dependent on me. He had his wife and children," he said.

After a while he added, "Sir, I was depressed for months after Venky passed away. The army doctor who treated me after this shock reported to my commandant that I should be allowed to get away from the sordid surroundings of Jaffna. However, I wanted to continue and avenge Venky's death. The senior officers overruled me and I was sent on long leave for an indefinite period. I am expected to appear before the Chief Medical Officer (CMO) of Pilibhit every month. His reports are the reason for my continued leave. Now, I feel I can go back. This morning I came to you to request you to speak to the CMO and secure an NOC for me."

"Roshan, you have come like a source of light today. You have lived up to the name that your parents have given you. Without your presence, I would have been a sitting duck for the militants who took a shot at me. I would have spoken to the CMO or your commandant for taking you back on active duty out of gratitude. However, after what I have heard from you today, I am not sure if you are emotionally ready to perform the tough duties which you will be assigned," I told him candidly.

"Sir, the IPKF is back in India. I will be on routine duties which are performed by the CRPF. Am I not fit even for that?" He quizzed.

I promptly shot back, "I would not like to influence the CMO's judgment. He is a medical professional and his opinion must be respected."

"Then, sir, please consider the possibility of allowing me to accompany you when you go into areas where militants are active. I assure you, I will not let any harm come to you. Sir, please give me this chance," he said imploringly.

"This is not possible as per rules. How can you be deployed here overlooking all the relevant rules of your force? Roshan, forget about this," I shot back.

"Sir, think about this. I could be an asset for the Pilibhit police with the experience that I have gathered in Sri Lanka and I hail from Bilsanda, which gives me a ringside view of militants in the area," was his parting sentence.

* * *

I continued to process the events that had transpired since the morning. The fact is that death had come calling, only to be averted by the most unusual circumstances. My mind went back to the stroll with Maanas whose life could have also been exposed to mortal danger. This realization sent a shiver down my spine. How many times does it happen that you are a hair's breadth away from a bullet which has your name written on it and someone descends like Superman to avert a sure-fire happening? The bravery shown by Roshan Singh was of the highest order. He had put his own life on the line. I thought that it was my duty to speak to his commandant and report the remarkable act of pluck performed by my saviour. This was the least I could have done for a hero like him.

A little later, I spoke to the DIG Range and IG Zone stationed at Bareilly. Both of them seemed to be incredulous. To my surprise, they appeared to be of the view that I was overreacting and things could not have been as bad as I had described. The IG went to the extent of advising me to respond 'maturely' to what had happened. He told me in no uncertain terms not to let the matter go beyond the boundary of the compound of the SP. He also instructed me not to have the matter recorded in writing or get an FIR registered. So, here I was, with my immediate superiors unwilling to take my word for it. Fortunately, the IG decided that the DIG would visit Pilibhit the same day to assess the situation. I was relieved at this decision. A couple of hours later, the DIG arrived. He inspected the scene of the incident. He admitted that all the evidence and the statements of those who were eyewitnesses, pointed to the occurrence of the incident as I had reported it. He left for Bareilly soon after, assuring me that he would apprise the IG of all the facts.

Later, in the evening, the IG was on the line once again. He agreed that the matter could not be brushed under the carpet. He assured me that he would convey the facts to the DGP and the government.

* * *

Reading the Signs

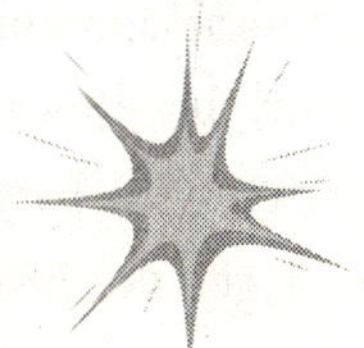

After the explosive visiting card that was delivered to me within days of my assuming charge in Pilibhit, I decided to strengthen the intelligence setup. In keeping with my time-tested method, I looked for sources from within the society, thus adding to the variety of informants.

My predecessor had introduced me to a friend of his who ran a business in Pilibhit. He told me that his friend, Ajay Agarwal, was a storehouse of information about the district and more particularly, about the town. I made a few inquiries to satisfy myself that I could depend on him for reliable information and concluded that Ajay was, indeed, very well informed and that he could be depended upon. He was in a trade which brought people from across the social spectrum to his establishment, a restaurant. Not surprisingly, he was aware of the sensational attack on me, despite my superiors thinking that an event like this could be kept under wraps.

Ajay was of the view that I needed to build bridges with the Sikh community. He told me about half a dozen members of the community who were trustworthy and enjoyed respect from all sections of the society.

One of the names he mentioned was of Sardar Sukhbir Singh Kohli. Ajay told me that Kohli was a farmer who was willing to diversify his agricultural operations and that he was not averse to experimenting with new developments in science and the progressive practices of drawing the best out of the farmland.

A couple of days after I got the heads-up about Kohli from Ajay, he visited my camp office. He turned out to be a man who was unapologetically voluble and every now and then, managed to slip humorous bits into his conversation. He had an infectious laugh that punctuated his conversation. It was delightful to see a man open up so much in the first meeting itself.

I estimated that Kohli was about eight to ten years older than me. I was grossly mistaken. It surprised me that he was actually more than twenty years in the lead. I wondered if it was his delightful disposition that kept him so young at heart or was there some other secret. I decided to ask him about his magic potion when we met next.

As if reading my thoughts, he came up voluntarily with an aspect of his personality. '*Lalji, apna to Faiz ki baat mein bharosa hai: aye kuchh abr kuchh sharaab aaye, uske baad aaye jo azaab aaye* (I believe the poet Faiz when he says: All I need to face life's challenges and difficulties is good weather and some alcohol).' He broke into an enormous belly laugh and added, "I have the best collection of alcohol in the town. Come some day and share those moments of bliss with me when the nectar of life is flowing!"

As he got up, I assured him that I was taking a raincheck on his invitation.

He turned to leave and then apparently recalled why he had come. He said, " Sir, I came to invite you to my house. I am holding a demonstration for my farmer friends the day after tomorrow on how to establish a business of rearing honey bees. I have been to a workshop recently and I think that Pilibhit has great potential to undertake bee-keeping."

I thought that this was a great offer from Kohli because it would give me the opportunity to develop contacts in the farming community. I said, "Sure, Kohli sahib, I will definitely come. It will be a chance to learn something new."

"Great! I will look forward to your presence. And don't call me sahib! I will prefer it if you call me by the name that my friends and family use – Sukhi...just Sukhi!"

I said I will keep his request in mind, but made a slip immediately when I said, "It was delightful to meet you, Kohli sahib... I mean Sukhi ji."

"Just Sukhi," he said, with a parting smile.

I went out into the veranda to see him off. I told him that I would come to his house in my private car and no policeman would accompany me. I also told him that I would be comfortable if I was allowed to mingle with others without being introduced as a police officer.

There was a look of disbelief on his face but he nodded.

* * *

I was at Nabi & Sons, a flute seller's shop, in Bashir Khan Lane. The lane joins with Lal Road in Pilibhit. The world-famous flutes crafted in Pilibhit had attracted me to this well-known shop. Buyers were making their selections in the shop and other outlets around it and in the process, playing a few notes on the flutes that they picked. The effect was a rush of discordant notes. In this musical chaos, there were some moments of divine beatific sounds, which had the power to take one into another world.

Mohammad Aftab Nabi, the genial octogenarian who ran the establishment with a passionate wavelength of pride, noticed that I was attentive to the music that was all around. He also sized up my discomfort at what can best be described as an unbearable pandemonium, in a lane dedicated to dreamy notes produced from one of the simplest, yet, amazingly mellifluous instruments.

"*Janab*, are you looking for a particular type of flute? We have a number of variants – directly-blown, rim-blown, end-blown and side-blown. What would be your preference?" queried Nabi.

"Nabi bhai, I do not play the instrument. It is just that I love music and when I listen to Pandit Hari Prasad Chaurasia's recital of Raga Des, I enter a world of bliss, leaving all my worries behind."

"My personal favourite is his *Hansadhwani*. It gives me the feeling as though I am flying in the clear blue sky, with a beautiful river winding its way through the verdant woods and I descend upon it to pick pearls from the depths of its water."

"You certainly have a vivid imagination. How do you tolerate all the noise around you? All the octaves that are simultaneously scaled in this lane must be irksome."

"I have been sitting in this place for over six decades. All that surrounds me has become a part of me. I feel as though I am a part of this milieu as well. I wonder if I will ever like it any other way." After a pause, he added, "I see greatness walk this lane so often. Pandit Hari Prasad ji has graced my shop more than once. I was a young man when Pannalal Ghosh visited us. Raghunath Seth also buys his flutes from this place. Among the youngsters, Ronu Majumdar prefers our flutes. I see a great future for him. He is only twenty-five years old, you know!" He drew my attention proudly to a number of pictures displayed in the shop, featuring some great flutists who bought their instruments from there.

One of his assistants came close to him and whispered, "I have noticed some strange-looking tall sardars in the Mohof forest. I don't think they are locals. I find their presence unsettling, Aftab *miyan*."

I could hear what was being whispered. It must have been because my ears are attuned to information which has a bearing on my profession. I thanked Nabi for the time he had given me and told him that I would visit again some other time.

"Janab, I am happy to meet someone who has an ear for music. Please visit my humble place again." After a pause, he asked, "Where do you live? I have not seen you before."

"I have come here recently. I am looking for suitable accommodation to make this place my home. I will take your leave." I deliberately avoided telling him my true identity. I wanted to remain incognito. That would help me walk around these crowded areas for picking first-hand buzz about the happenings in the town.

The information about the presence of unidentified outsiders had led to my decision to leave Bashir Khan Lane in a hurry.

As I drove off in my Maruti 800 car, I decided to take a detour and return to my camp office only after skirting the side of the forest that the shopkeeper had mentioned. I drove around at a slow speed and decided to halt at a couple of places to crane my neck for any suspicious signs that I could decipher. At one point, I got out of the car and stood behind a large sal tree as if to relieve myself. I looked around as far as I could in the mist-laden thick forest. I noticed that about two hundred metres inside the forest, there was a fire that had died out but still had smoke rising from it. I surmised that this must have been a fire that was lit by the sardars who were seen by the shopkeeper. The day was freezing cold and it must have been a big challenge to endure the early morning temperature. I stayed for close to an hour in the vicinity of the forest to see if there were any other signs of an unwelcome presence. I did not have a wireless set, so I could not ask any other officers to join me. I decided that what I had overheard at Nabi's shop could not be ignored and deserved urgent attention.

On returning to my office, I issued instructions to the SHO and LIU to keep a close eye on the Mohof Range area.

***

The international border between India and Nepal has a stretch of nearly fifty-five kilometres in Pilibhit district. Passport-free travel is permitted between the two countries and the porosity of the border makes the task of security challenging. It was essential for me to study this area first-hand, so that I could attempt to plug some of the weak links.

I undertook a whirlwind tour of these border areas to understand where we were lacking in our strategy, resources and preparedness. The posts that I visited were beset with daunting tasks. The temperatures ranged from sub-zero in the winter to over forty in the summer. There was extreme humidity in the lead-up to the monsoon season, followed by heavy rains. One should also not forget that the wildlife here included predators of the most dangerous kind and the deadliest reptiles as well as insects. Malarial mosquitoes were another common menace. When I visited the interior posts, it was touching to experience the hospitality of the personnel who performed duties in such uninhabitable circumstances. The tea and biscuits that they offered to me must have been mustered by them after painstaking efforts. It is for such bits of warmth that one becomes completely sucked into the police culture. People often ask me what forms the strong bond that they see between policemen of all ranks. My answer is that it is these seemingly trifling acts that hold the magic.

Attached to some of these posts were officials of the LIU and the state intelligence also had a presence in a couple of places. I had discussions with these officials and was soon abreast of what they had gathered. I stressed on the importance of the international border from the point of view of the activities of Sikh militants who had been noticed in certain parts of the district. I considered the possibility that there might be hideouts where the militants coming from Punjab or the ones that were being pursued in our jurisdiction, might find shelter. Much to my relief, no such input was available till that point in time.

During this trip, I made a stop at a beautiful rest house of the irrigation department at Banbasa on the banks of the Sharda Canal. I was enjoying the morning sun when a young boy met me. He told me about the adverse circumstances which his village folk, more particularly his own family, were facing.

"What brings you here, Balvinder?" I enquired of the young Sikh boy, who was barely fifteen years old.

He looked over his shoulder and then, spoke to me in a low voice, "Uncle ji, I live in the village Pistaur which is close to Amaria. The entire population there belongs to my community. We have been living there since the time of our ancestors. My grandfather was born here soon after his family had shifted to this village."

He paused for a moment and then resumed, "Uncle ji, my forefathers have worked very hard in this inhospitable terrain. They have braved multiple challenges and established a prosperous farming operation. Not only are we living in comfortable circumstances, we have also employed a number of men for farm work. We provide employment to more than two dozen people."

"Then, what exactly is the problem, Balvinder?"

Once again, Balvinder seemed to check with furtive glances that what he was telling me was not being heard by ears other than mine. He moved closer to me and whispered, "There are outsiders who come to the *jhala* and ask for food and money. They even insist that they will need accommodation to stay. They pointed out the room on the upper floor as the one they will definitely like to use. Sir, I mean Uncle ji, I have seen those men carrying dangerous weapons, the kind which I have only seen in films. They have threatened that they will kill everyone in our family if we say anything about their movements to the police."

"Who are the people living in your *jhala*?"

"All of them are our relatives. There are only seven houses and about sixty of us. Yes, there are a few servants and farmhands also."

After a while, he added, "There are young girls at whom these outsiders look with glances about which I overheard my parents talk. They are worried that these girls are no longer safe in the *jhala*. I do not know what exactly is bothering my father and mother but it appears to be a serious concern. You will have to reach out to them to understand their mind. But the whole *jhala* is scared to be seen with anyone from the police."

I thought for a while before responding, "Okay, Balvinder. Thank you for the input. You have alerted me to a gathering storm. I will take effective action and ensure that no harm comes to anyone in your *jhala*. Go back to your parents and tell them about our meeting. I am sure they will be relieved. I admire you for having come to me. You are a brave boy, just as we expect from the members of your community."

"Thank you, Uncle ji. You can call me Ballu. That is the name I prefer to hear from people whom I can trust."

"Okay, Ballu." I smiled.

* * *

Sukhi was in his true element. The ten or fifteen farmers who had gathered at his house to learn about the latest techniques of bee-keeping were being treated to a barrage of jokes. The language being employed was Punjabi, but the dialect he was using was noticeably at variance from what I was used to. On most occasions, I could understand what was being said in Punjabi, but Sukhi's language was largely Greek to me. As he saw me approach the group, his immediate reaction was one of visible excitement. I had the feeling that he was about to give me a hug as long-lost friends would. Fortunately, he seemed to have recalled my request to keep my participation low-key. He just said a simple '*Sat Sri Akal*' and shook my hand perfunctorily. Moments later, the interaction veered to the topic of the day – bee-keeping.

While Sukhi was explaining the essential difference to distinguish an *Apis andreniformis* from an *Apis florea* or an *Apis cerana* from an *Apis dorsata*, my attention was negligible to what was being said. I was observing those who were present, one after the other and trying to understand their characteristics as well as body language. I was optimistic that some of those present would be aware of the movement of armed militants in different parts of the district. Was it possible to spot likely sources of information in this group?

I was drawn instinctively to a portly young man who showed great interest in what was being said. He was also asking some questions which demonstrated his eagerness to learn from Sukhi. I found another person to be interesting as well. Tall and middle-aged, he was wearing a tracksuit and taking notes on an electronic diary. A distinguished-looking man, probably in his seventies, was impressively erect and alert during the entire session. He asked only one, though pertinent, question, "What is the difference in the properties of the honey gathered during different seasons of the year and why is there a difference in the price of honey that is gathered from different species of bees?"

Sukhi was the perfect teacher and most willing to share whatever knowledge he had. I was impressed by his ability to enthuse those present, to learn from him about new methods for multiplying the income from their farms. As the interaction ended, the participants gathered around a table where the latest models of hives were displayed. Sukhi was explaining which one was more suitable for apiaries in rural settings and which hives would be more appropriate for urban spaces. I had little interest in this knowledge but my observation of the men who were gathered there was keeping me engaged.

Sukhi announced with a degree of pomp, "Friends, we have a highly distinguished guest present here." As he said this, my heart sank and I wished that I had some way of becoming invisible. I thought that Sukhi was going to spill the beans. He started to move towards where I was standing. My heart skipped many beats as he stopped just behind me. I was relieved when I heard him say, "Meet Professor Darbara Singh!" He kept his hand on the shoulder of the man standing next to me – a move which brought my tension down by several notches. "It is a matter of great pride for Pilibhit that a man of his learning and expertise is visiting us. He is an expert in dairy management and I have requested him to stay for a few days, study our dairy farms and give us valuable tips on how to improve our operations." The professor was the one who had asked the question about the difference in the honey gathered in different seasons. While he was acknowledging the greetings of the others, I quietly moved away to a place that was not too close to the professor, lest he asked me to introduce myself.

Tea, *lassi* and an impressive spread of snacks were offered next. I had the feeling that at least two pairs of eyes were focussed on me repeatedly – those of the professor and the other of the portly young man I had noticed earlier.

* * *

A couple of days later, Sukhi was in my office. Accompanying him was Professor Darbara Singh. Sukhi was his usual chirpy self while the professor was maintaining a dignified silence. His only contributions to the conversation came in the form of nods or monosyllables. I wanted him to open up because I found his reserved demeanour to be unsettling. I needed to learn more about him, especially his views of the ongoing incidents involving militants.

"Professor, I am glad to have met you the other day at Sukhi's place." I asked, by way of breaking ice. "I am sure that you will impart important tips to the dairy farmers to improve their techniques and increase the output of milk. Could you throw some light on what you have observed and how the processes could be streamlined?"

"I am still trying to make sense of what the local farmers want, to what extent are they willing to try new techniques, what are the problems that they might encounter and in what way is the government prepared to extend monetary and infrastructural support." This was the longest sentence I had heard the professor speak and, I must add, he made sense.

"I will need to travel to a number of villages and meet farmers, in order to assess their willingness to adopt progressive dairy farming techniques."

"That is so wonderful. In case you happen to learn about it, we would like to get an input from you on the impact of the violent incidents involving suspected Sikh militants."

The expression on the professor's face changed and I thought that it betrayed a little loss of composure. I tried to interpret the observation in my mind. Only moments later, the elderly visitor's face assumed, what by then, was my idea of his normal expression.

Sukhi and Darbara Singh left a few minutes later. The former proffered a warm handshake with the affability that I had come to associate with him. He said, "I have received a bottle of Jack Daniel's from my cousin who lives in Canada. Please come over for a drink." The Professor's handshake was merely a formal one, limp and missing in spirit. He forced a fake smile on his face.

Darbara Singh's demeanour during our meeting was stuck in my thoughts. Why was he so reserved? Why did he come across as someone who wasn't friendly? Did he really have the intention of spreading knowledge in the domain of dairy farming or was there some hidden agenda too? I couldn't dismiss my instinct that the old professor needed to be kept under watch. The policeman in me was knocking.

The same evening, I decided to drop in at Sukhi's place. He received me at the gate of his sprawling residence with his usual exuberance. His wife was also at the gate to welcome me.

"So wonderful to have you over, *Kaptan* sahib. I know that little Maanas is slightly under the weather and I had told Jaspreet that you may come alone." He looked at his wife as he spoke and Jaspreet nodded. She added, "Do tell me if *Bhabhiji* needs any help. I'll come and look her up soon."

As we made ourselves comfortable and Jaspreet had gone to the kitchen, I spoke to Sukhi, "How long have you known Professor Darbara Singh?"

"I have met him only a few days ago. A friend of mine, Simranjit, who has a business of arranging pilgrimage tours for Sikhs living in Canada and other countries, told me about him. He suggested that the professor's expertise could be exploited to bring prosperity to farmers. I am glad that the professor has dived headlong into work," he said, with a look of triumph.

Sukhi was in his element as he described Tennessee's famous brew which we were sharing, "Sir, do you know? Until 1987, Jack Daniel's Black Label was produced at 90 U.S. proof, which is equivalent to 45% alcohol by volume. The lower-end green label product was 80 proof. However, starting in 1987, the other label variations also were reduced in proof. So, the Black Label that we are enjoying is of the lower proof." Saying so, he quickly gulped down the peg that he was holding. I could assess that he was now a little under the influence of the spirit that he was consuming, which prompted him to show off his knowledge. I thought that this would be a good time to ask more about the professor.

"Sukhi, has the professor told you about his plans for popularising modern dairy farming?'"

"He asked me about some Sikhs who wield influence. He said that he plans to go to the Sikhs who have money and could be relied upon to contribute generously for just causes."

"Did you give him such names?"

'Yes, I gave him about a dozen names."

"Where is he now?"

"He must be in some *jhala* in village Khandepur, under the Pooranpur police station area. The list that I gave him included a few names from that area."

In the meantime, Sukhi had downed another peg and his inebriation was pronounced.

I asked him, "Sukhi, do you find anything unusual in the way the professor behaves? Isn't he a bit too reserved?"

I had to repeat my question in order to focus Sukhi's attention to what I was saying. He contemplated before he answered, "I find him a big bore, sir! Not my kind at all." He laughed and added, "Had it not been for Simranjit, I would not have entertained him. Let us hope he delivers on his promise of improving the lot of our farmer friends."

"Sukhi, please give me the names that you have shared with the professor."

I obtained the names from him. As I left Sukhi's house, I started wondering if I could place my complete trust in him.

"Babuji, please ask the inspector, LIU to come immediately," I asked my steno, on reaching the camp office at my residence. It was late in the evening, yet, I thought that I may sleep more peacefully if instructions were passed on to the person who would bring vital input for my plans to be put in place, before I retired for the day.

* * *

It was about midnight when LIU Inspector Shiv Shankar Yadav arrived. He preferred to be called SS. I often wondered why he preferred this address to his surname. I decided to ask him why. I was surprised by his answer. He said, “Sir, I am like the German SS. I am confident that I look even smarter than my colleagues who wear a uniform and I am loyal to my superiors like committed soldiers are.”

I smiled and asked him if he knew what the dreaded Schutzstaffel, abbreviated SS, supported. He was not even vaguely aware that it was a key component in the rise of Hitler and the Nazis, virtually a state within a state. I could see that on hearing this, much of his enthusiasm for being called SS had whittled down.

I gave him the list given to me by Sukhi and explained its significance to him. I said, “I do not find Professor Darbara Singh to be someone who can be taken at face value. SS, I want you to tap your information sources in the Sikh families of the villages which figure on the professor’s itinerary. This has to be kept utterly confidential and the subject must not get a whiff.”

“Yes sir, I understand. I have reliable sources in at least two of these villages. I will put Pritam Pal on the job to dig out more.”

“Good idea. Pritam Pal is a resourceful person with useful contacts in his community,” I said about the young Sikh intelligence officer.

"*Aur koi hukum*, sir?"

"*Nahin*, get down to work immediately, SS."

"Jai Hind, sir."

The inspector turned to leave. After taking a couple of steps, he turned back and said, "Sir, call me Yadav. Or Shiv Shankar. Not SS. Please, sir."

As Yadav left, I once again went back to my concern if Sukhi could be relied upon completely.

* * *

In the days that followed my late-night meeting with the LIU inspector, I got intel from him which supported my worst fears. In none of the meetings that he held in the Pooranpur, Neoria, Umaria, Gajraula and Bilsanda police station areas did the professor discuss dairy farming. His meetings were held behind closed doors and not attended by anyone other than those whose names figured on the list we had. Four of those whom the professor met, were in touch with police officers soon after and gave details of the agenda. From their accounts, it was clear that the old man was on a mission to collect funds and his appeal for fat donations was based on the dream of establishing a Khalistan that was free from India. The funds were required for waging a long war with the Indian state which, according to him, was responsible for crushing the just demands for a separate country for the followers of the *Khalsa Panth*. He had advocated extreme methods for the purpose, including acts of terror to keep the governments in New Delhi and Lucknow on the defensive. His theory was that not only Punjab, but also a long tract including the Terai area falling in the state of Uttar Pradesh, fell rightfully under the territories of Khalistan that he envisaged as the land for the true followers of Sikhism. He wanted *jathas* of devout Sikhs to travel to the Golden Temple in Amritsar to take oath and accept *amrit* from the priests there to devote themselves to the Khalsa cause.

Any doubts about Darbara Singh were put to rest. Our intel and the information readily provided by the local Sikh farmers unambiguously pointed towards only one conclusion. He was a Khalistan activist who had sought the participation of influential local Sikhs to join the movement for a separate Sikh land.

We did not waste any time. We took Professor Darbara Singh into our custody within hours of a meeting that he held in the Bilsanda area. I directed the best sleuths working on the Khalistan militancy to deal with him. As it turned out, Darbara Singh had returned from Canada with dreams of establishing a separate country for Sikhs. He had the backing of some Canada-based groups that were sympathetic to the cause. He had come to Pilibhit on the invitation of some active militants, the most notable of whom was one the police had given the name Mark Stallion. It is to be noted that the dreaded Mark Stallion had come to light even earlier, when I was the SP in Shahjahanpur district. The most important takeaway from his interrogation was the identification of the likely hideouts of Mark Stallion.

The interrogation of Darbara Singh helped us identify some of the active criminals who were involved in militant activities supporting the Khalistan movement. Our gang charts were accordingly updated.

***

In the meantime, all doubts about Sukhi had been conclusively put to rest. The fact that he had provided the list of those with whom the professor was likely to hold a meeting most readily pointed to his non-involvement. It was supported by the fact that he had invited me for an introduction to the local farmers, when the professor had come to his residence. He had also brought him to my office, which underlined his complete ignorance about the professor's involvement in the militant movement.

Yet, as a matter of extra caution, I deployed intelligence personnel to keep a watch on him. It was risky to ignore any signals.

***

Mark Stallion

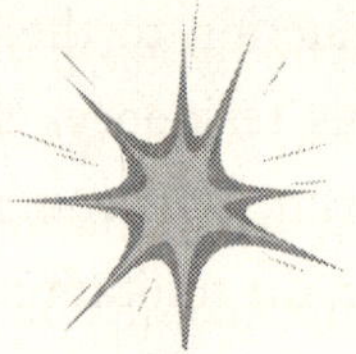

Leaders come in all shapes and sizes. Some blaze a trail which remains the guiding light for generations to follow. Their leadership styles are the subject of umpteen discussions; a number of scholarly theses are written to understand the finer points that make them special. Children are exhorted to follow their examples. Songs are written to extol their unmatched virtues. They leave the world a better place through their great leadership and virtues. They become household names. Folklore abounds with their exploits. Gandhiji can be safely counted as one such leader.

What makes the leaders of criminal gangs acquire cult status? Their detestable acts are unscrupulous and violent, yet, why do some of them become legends? Why do any number of literary and other creative works have these characters central to their stories? New entrants into the dark arena draw inspiration from these villains. They are even studied by scholars and psychologists to come up with findings that throw light on their rise to leadership positions. The media headlines scream about their depredations. There are exaggerations at times, yet, it is the sensational nature of their acts that catches the public eye. Mark Stallion was one such leader. He was a 'General' of the Bhindranwale Tiger Force (BTF) and a torchbearer for the Khalistan movement after the elimination of many of his compatriots in Operation Blue Star.

When I took over the reins of the Pilibhit police, this name was on everyone's lips. News items were built around his impact on the ongoing militancy in the Terai districts. His crimes committed in Punjab carried their tales ahead of him when he shifted his operations to Uttar Pradesh. In at least four districts, the police were on their toes. The preparedness to meet an operator of his scale, training levels, infrastructure, weaponry and above all, the intelligence about him, were all reasons for worry.

The media was more concerned about its TRP than a sober and fact-based account of Mark Stallion's change of operational area. He was being described in terms which helped him build a reputation of invincibility, cunningness and such a dramatic level of gumption, that even the most efficient and best-informed police officers developed a complex. Long lists of his crime history were being quoted right, left and centre, without a responsible fact-checking process. The public at large rarely doubted these reports.

A larger-than-life image bolstered the militant leader's clout and the operatives in the Terai districts accepted him as someone superior. He managed to sneak into Terai with four of his men of confidence. He possessed superior firepower, thanks to a couple of AK rifles, for which he was looked up to as an asset, in creating conditions suitable for carrying out the nefarious programme of the militants and boosting the K-cause.

Mark Stallion created an aura around what was primarily a weakness: his relocation to UP after his survival. He managed to give the impression that it was a deliberate move on his part to shift his area of operations whereas the reality was that he was lucky to have escaped the dragnet of the Punjab forces at a time when the militants were under intense pressure and one after the other was being accounted for. The word was spread that his operations in Terai were to emphasise the claim of the Khalistan supporters on the territories of this area too.

My assessment of his weaknesses was based on what was pretty obvious – his base in Pilibhit was not founded on the local support of the Sikhs of the district. In fact, they were opposed to the separatist sentiment and were steadfast in their allegiance to the country. They were loath to join a movement which lacked sentimental appeal for them. They were shocked by the Operation Blue Star, but were not willing to connect it to the call of certain elements, who advocated a break from the Indian union and creating Khalistan as a separate entity for Sikhs. Consequently, there was no connect of the local population with the militants.

The desperados were, thus, employing strong-arm tactics to force hospitality on unwilling hosts. The threats held out to them were of serious retribution, should they not provide shelter, food or money. These unwelcome guests needed to keep their image of being unscrupulous killers intact, so they would unhesitatingly eliminate such persons who appeared to be informers of the local authorities. '...terrorists in Terai gunned down five people – all members of local Sikh families - on suspicion that they were police informers. Four of the victims, including a woman, were killed in three separate incidents in Pilibhit, where the police have made large arms seizures in the last couple of months.' Their trigger happiness extended to bumping off those as well who resisted the payment of money to them.

Another development was that some women were reportedly becoming victims of sexual advances. Women were, therefore, feeling unsafe. The honour of the families was constantly threatened.

For the above reasons, I felt that our local police officers were in a position to create reliable sources of information from among the Sikh residents.

However, the threat of the militants which gripped the locals could not be underestimated. It was, indeed, a well-understood fact that the methods employed by the outlaws follow no rules of justice, while the police had no option but to go by the book. The choice was between putting one's life on the line and facing legal action for giving shelter to the militants. The immediate threat was proving to be too much of a risk for them and depending on the police for protection carried its own pitfalls.

In one case, 'a police picket tried to stop a tractor-trailer at the Dudhiya Khurd railway station, ten kilometres from Puranpur tehsil of Pilibhit. The occupants fired at the picket and fled, abandoning the tractor.'

This was an act of bravado which displayed the spunk of those who were intent on creating an atmosphere of terror. The act became even more alarming because the ownership of the tractor was traced to a local farmer of Panpur. The owner offered a hefty bribe to get the seized tractor released. The owner's offer made the police even more suspicious and they launched a more intensive search of the vehicle.

The search of the tractor-trailer revealed a concealed cache of deadly weaponry. The police arrested the owner and his son for harbouring terrorists. On investigation, it came to light that Mark Stallion had brought the trolley from Punjab, loaded it on a truck and then got hold of the tractor that was later recovered by the police.

The Mark Stallion gang had clearly made its presence felt in the region. Stallion himself led a raid on the State Bank of India branch in Gola Gokarnath in the year 1989 and shot dead a guard. The police learnt that he had brought in a fresh supply of arms, including rockets, to replenish his armoury around the same time.

Mark Stallion had created a colossal impact when he threatened a police informer with death and actually carried out the threat by killing his whole family in the Phool Behar village of the neighbouring district Kheri. The word went around that he had carried out this heinous act in the presence of the police. Highly exaggerated versions of such daredevil acts travelled to far off locations and added to the unconquerable persona of the man.

The Sikhs who were living in Terai were facing threats from both sides – the militants were forcing them to extend help to them in varying manners and the police looked at them with suspicion for providing logistical support. It was a time when even highly respectable Sikhs were feeling like children of lesser gods.

The legend of Mark Stallion was not debilitating only for the local residents; it dented police morale as well.

My job was well-defined. I had to work to bring life back on track for the people and re-establish the rule of law by unquestionably resuming the eroded writ of the police.

* * *

Behind the Lens

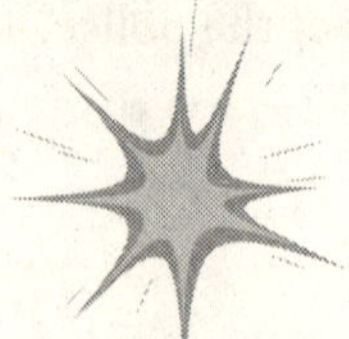

The sharp downpour of the morning had bathed all the surroundings. Everything looked as if it were fresh out of nature, especially the beautiful blue sky, interspersed with white cotton-like cumulus clouds and the proud sal trees that seemed to be celebrating their verdant glory. I could feel the wind on my face and there was a very light, almost quiet rustling of leaves. Small wavelets began to form in a pond next to which I stood. As Mohammad Rafi's mesmerising voice expressed my feelings, '*Dil Kahe Ruk Ja O Ruk Ja Yahin Pe Kahin…*' (The heart yearns to stay here… somewhere here only…) on the car cassette player, I had at the back of my mind the urgency to go back to my camp office where I had convened a meeting to discuss our strategy for the week in our on-going operations.

I had to pick up some stationery on the way back, so I stopped at a store. I was waiting for my stuff to be packed and casually looked outside to notice that the buzz in the street was increasing. I also noticed that there was a photographer who was focusing his lens on my car. I could not have overlooked this activity. It was unusual for people to click photographs without a purpose. In 1991, the now ubiquitous phone cameras had not appeared. Cameras used to be noticeable gadgets and someone taking a photograph of my car was enough to raise my hackles.

I quickly concluded that the stationery could wait. It was more important for me to check out the lens-man. I rushed out and quietly made my way behind him. I tapped on his shoulder and he looked back. As he saw me, he panicked and tried to run away. I had foreseen such a possibility and was prepared to prevent him from doing so. I had taken off my belt which I threw around him quickly and jolted it strongly to bring him down on the pavement. I snatched his camera, which hung from his neck, in the same movement and I was now standing above the man. In the meantime, I had also pulled out my revolver which I pointed at him. Now, I felt sufficiently in control of the situation to tell him to stand up. I caught him by his collar from behind and put the revolver menacingly on his back. I told him to move to the police outpost Khakra, which was barely a few metres away. He complied and made no further attempt to escape. As I reached the outpost, one of the men recognised me and saluted. The other policemen on duty immediately took stock of the situation and understood its seriousness.

The man in my captivity looked at me with a different attitude now and spoke for the first time, "Sir, I did not know who you were. I would never have tried to take a photograph of your car. I was ordered to do so by Inder, the owner of the photo studio for which I work."

"Did he not tell you why this photo was to be taken?"

"No. He just pointed out the car to me. After that, he went away from the spot."

"What is your name?"

"Sunil, sir."

I told the officer in-charge of the Khakra outpost to bring Inder from wherever he could be located. I also directed that both Sunil and Inder be brought to my camp office, so that I could grill the two men with the help of the other officers.

Before I departed for my camp office, I picked up the stationery that I had selected at the shop. As I collected the stuff, the shop owner expressed his appreciation for my swift action and said that the whole market now recognised the new SP of the district.

The news had already travelled to my office when I reached there and I received unsolicited advice from my official driver, Lallan Yadav, "Sir, even if you go to town in your private car, please use the services of a police driver. It is even better if the gunner is also with you."

Amarjit, my gunner, also joined in to add, "Sir, you never know when these desperados will attack. I must get the chance to protect you when such a thing happens."

By now, the officers who were to attend the meeting had started to arrive. All of them looked alarmed which made me realize that the news of the incident in the market had reached them too.

I asked the additional SP, "You seem to have learned about the incident. Is that the reason why you are perturbed?"

"Yes sir, not only me, but the whole town is talking about it. I hope you are not injured," Yashbir Bisht, the additional SP enquired.

"No, I am fine. Let us ask why he found my Maruti so click-worthy." All of us went into my office and I asked for the persons who were making the day's news, Sunil and Inder, to be sent in, one by one. Deputy SP Shivdan Singh and SHO Haleem Khan had also joined us by then.

* * *

Sunil, a short, sickly man who appeared to be under intense pressure of some kind, held Inder, his employer, solely responsible for what had happened. He said "Sir, I am a poor servant. Inder had given me the simple task of capturing a photo of the car and told me that I should quickly click the photograph and leave the place immediately."

"Then why did you try to run away when I patted you on your shoulder?"

"Sir, the manner in which he gave me the order had made me suspicious. He was clearly nervous and did not want to remain on the spot. I wondered why he had not done the job himself."

"But you took a few minutes to complete the simple task. Wasn't that too long a time?"

"Yes sir, the haste with which I had to take the shot made me nervous, so I became unsure about the mechanism of the camera. When you accosted me, I was struggling with the shutter button which I had accidentally locked in that state of confusion. I had not clicked a single picture of the car till then."

In the meantime, the film in his camera had been developed by the police photographer.

The pictures were mostly of a professional level. Some, however, were of a lesser quality. I found that there were some photographs that had been taken in a studio while others had been shot at location. One Sikh man featured repeatedly in them. Some of the locations were well-known spots in the district. Among them were Chuka Beach, Bifurcation and the Brahmachari Ghat temple. The last of these is located in the Khakra *mohalla,* the locality where the morning incident had occurred.

I noticed that the Sikh man who was seen in half a dozen snaps seemed to be a pompous person. His manner exhibited his tendency to show-off what he thought were his best angles. In two of the pictures, one at Chuka Beach and the other at Bifurcation, he was displaying an AK-47 rifle. This made this character a person of interest for us.

"Sunil, who is this gentleman?" I enquired.

Sunil looked closely at the picture and then shook his head to convey that he did not know who the man was. I raised my voice to a menacing level and signalled the SHO to give him an idea of the extent to which we could go to get him to answer the question. SHO Haleem Khan was known for his ability to prise out the truth from under any number of impregnable layers. Without doubt, his methods were rather direct. All he did to give a taste of what to expect was to firmly put his foot clad in ammunition boots on Sunil's foot and press it down with a force that seemed adequate to crush the emaciated man's toes. Sunil's cry of pain would have shaken the entire building.

"I will tell you, sir! I will...," he said, as he cried aloud.

Haleem removed his foot and looked at me to see if there was an expression of appreciation there. I am sure he must have been inconclusive in his assessment for I had tried to remain as inscrutable as possible.

"Okay, tell us. Who is this sardar?"

"Sir, all I know about him is that he is not from Pilibhit. He has come here recently. He came to our studio a couple of times. He speaks only Punjabi and I cannot understand much of what he says. He has never spoken to me but I have heard him talking to Inder who has a working knowledge of Punjabi."

"What was he saying to Inder?"

"He was talking about his photoshoot. On two occasions, Inder accompanied him on the Bullet that this sardar rode. I do not know where they had gone. I can see a couple of snaps that have been clicked in our studio too."

"Do you know anything more that you should share about this sardar?"

"I am afraid not, sir. Inder may be able to give you more information."

I signalled Haleem to show Sunil the way to the guard room and bring Inder from there after about fifteen minutes.

* * *

The officers present with me gave their individual assessments of the interrogation. One thing in which they were unanimous was that the effort to catch Sunil wasn't fruitless. There was promise in what we had learned from him. This was a good beginning.

When Haleem returned, he minced no words when he spoke about the outcome of the grilling, “Sir, too much *sharafat* will get us nowhere. Give Sunil to me, I’ll make the bastard cough up a lot more. *Saala bahut seedha ban raha hai*!”

I smiled but responded with silence. He was once again trying to read my face and understand what I thought of his proposal.

A few minutes later, the tall and portly Inder was ushered in. As he entered, he looked around the room and then jumped at the feet of the SHO saying, “Sir, you know me very well. I was the photographer at your son’s birthday party. I am a law-abiding simple man, sir. There has been some misunderstanding.” It was amusing to find that the mammoth Inder had a soft, almost feminine voice.

I nodded at Haleem to follow me into an anteroom.

“Do you know Inder?”

‘Sir, most of the officers of the police and other government departments know him. He is often asked to take photographs on official and private occasions. So far, I have not known anything adverse about him.”

“Then, do one thing. As we put questions to him, pretend as if you are sympathetic with him. Let him feel as though you are a friend. This time, I will behave roughly. Naturally, that will trigger similar behaviour from Shivdan and Yashbir too.”

Haleem nodded. After a while he said, “Sir, he should also be made a *hawai jahaz*.”

I smiled because I knew what he meant. He was suggesting that Inder should also be given a dose of the third-degree treatment.

I returned to the room where the interrogation was to be carried out. By now, the stout Inder was quivering from fear. He was sweating profusely in that cold weather and from his manner, it seemed that his colossal hundred-kilogram frame would collapse on the ground. I gave him a cold stare and he started to wail as if he had been hit hard. Haleem consoled him, "Don't worry, Kaptan sahib is kind-hearted. He will not hurt you. Just answer a few questions and you can go back home."

Inder's wailing did not stop, but he collected himself a little. Haleem offered him a chair into which the six-foot plus frame sank with gratitude.

He calmed down a lot after a glass of water was offered to him. It was a revelation for him to see Haleem in the *avatar* of a 'friend'.

"Sir, that man calls himself Sheru. He boasts all the time that he is the tiger of Punjab and claims to be invincible. He has visited my shop on more than one occasion in the last two weeks. I had never seen him in Pilibhit before this. He offered a handsome price for the photographs that he wanted me to take for him. He took me to a few well-known places in the district for being photographed. He spoke endlessly, but said nothing about the place from where he came or the business that brought him to Pilibhit." After a pause, Inder continued, "I concluded that he was a gasbag and dismissed his boastful ramblings. I carried on with the photoshoots he was so fond of, since after all, the services I was providing to him were being well-rewarded."

"Didn't you smell a rat somewhere? No one would be so profligate without any reason. Don't think that we are going to buy your cock-and-bull story without suspecting your role in it," I said with an expression that conveyed to him that we were going to employ a no-holds-barred manner in prising the truth out of him. As if to further drill down the message, I used a little of my limited vocabulary of the unprintable to accompany the potent threats.

My outburst emboldened Yashvir to come up with his own rich volley of the unprintable. I could not suppress the admiration I felt for the creativity that he displayed in weaving together profanities, which in some of the back alleys would have enjoyed the status of literary ingenuity!

The pressure on Inder was kept at a level which brought him to a breaking point. The team of interrogators experienced debilitating fatigue too. After a gruelling four hours of grilling, we reaped rewards. As we had expected, the burly photographer was now dripping with nuggets of information, on which we could feast with glee. It was as if his memory had been restored after he had received some well-known 'treatment' from us. This was the reward we had foreseen and had kept us going.

* * *

The upshot of Inder's revelations was that Sheru was not only a narcissistic man, he had relocated himself to Pilibhit to evade the dragnet of the Punjab police. It was Sheru who was responsible for the logistics of the militants who had come to Pilibhit and some other locations in Terai. He had contacts with certain Khalistan sympathisers in Canada as well as other foreign countries and his most significant contribution to the militants who were active in these areas was to provide finances.

We considered Sheru to be a great source of information. Our crusade against the militants would get a much-needed shot in the arm. We would be in a position to update our gang charts with the names of some unwanted outstation guests who were forcing themselves on what was essentially a peace-loving Sikh community.

We asked Inder to get Sheru for us. His immediate response was one of utter helplessness. "Sir, please believe me. I have no idea of his whereabouts," he pleaded.

"Then, how is it that he gets in touch with you and you join him for his photoshoots?"

"Sir, it is at his initiative that we meet at the places which he decides. I have never had a say in it."

"Of course, he must be sending someone to contact you, pick you up and take you to the locations. Tell us about these people who contact you."

Inder was thus cornered to tell us about the vital link between him and Sheru.

He was silent for a few minutes. He appeared to be in contemplation as if he was trying to recall something.

Suddenly, Shivdan shouted at the top of his voice, "*Saale, yaad dilaoon tujhe*? I know a very good method to jog your memory." Saying so, he picked up a stick and advanced threateningly towards Inder. Before anyone could react, he landed a resounding blow of the stick across Inder's thighs, followed by two more on each of his calves. The photographer started shouting and crying in pain and said, "*Batata hoon*. I know only one name, Jassi. He had come once to pick me up from my studio. I remember only his name."

"Where does Jassi live?"

"Sir, Jassi lives near my house in *gali* Phulkewali, close to Sri Brajwasi High School."

"Describe him."

"He is a short and emaciated man, in his early twenties."

"What does he do?"

"I have no idea, but I know that his father has a sweet shop."

"Where is the shop? What is it called?"

"Sir, the shop is in front of Brijwasi High School. It is called 'Sri Krishna Mishthan Bhandar'."

"Where can we find Jassi at this time? Does he mind the shop?"

"He seldom goes to the sweet shop. It seems that he does not get on well with his father."

"How do you know this?"

"His father has complained to me about Jassi's waywardness and asked me to counsel him."

I joined the conversation saying, "Waywardness? What is it that is so described by Jassi's father?"

"Sir, he does not work at the shop. He is not interested in studies and is generally a footloose kind of person. He seems to while away his time doing nothing useful. He has a motorcycle which he appears to love more than anything."

"Where does he get the money to buy petrol?"

"I have no idea. I know that his father does not indulge him."

"No idea? Now, do you once again need a dose from Deputy sahib to help you recall the source of Jassi's pocket money?" Saying so, I looked at Shivdan from the corner of my eye to find him becoming animated. He seemed to be itching to use the stick which he wielded threateningly. I gestured to him to calm down because his intent had brought about the desired response.

"Sir, I think he has something to do with criminals. He surely has some dubious sources for earning money."

"Any particular criminals? Name a few."

After much persuasion, cajoling, harsh words carrying ominous warnings, spine-chilling threats and Shivdan's potent doses, we made a few important breakthroughs. We now had half a dozen names which were enough to serve as the foundation for building a body of information related to criminals who were either members of militant gangs or active helpers. We also obtained leads to Jassi's likely locations.

* * *

Astabal

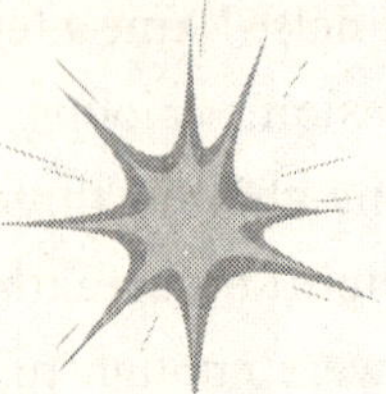

"Aloke, can you spend some more time with Maanas and me? I feel that you are too engrossed in crime and criminals, which must be drab and exhausting. I want you to go to work with a warm feeling."

Madhu was right. I knew that Pilibhit was proving to be an assignment that placed much more punishing demands on my time than other stations.

I picked up Maanas in my lap and asked Madhu to join the two of us in a family huddle. Soon after, I said to her, "I will be gone for an important follow-up of the work in which we were engaged for the last few days. I promise that I will not stay away for even a moment more than what is essential."

I could see that my wife's responding smile conveyed the lack of credibility she attached to such promises made by me. As I came out, my gunner, Amarjeet, reminded me that the other officers were waiting for a meeting at the office. I informed him that my programme had been revised and I was heading for the police lines[13] instead.

As I signalled the driver, Lallan Yadav to leave, he said, "Sir, a young boy wants to meet you. I told him that you were leaving for a meeting, but he said that it was urgent. Would you like to meet him?"

"I must leave. Okay, I will explain it to the boy myself." Saying so, I got down from the car and waited for the boy to be brought to me.

"O Ballu, it's you! I am elated to see you," I said having felt genuinely glad to see him.

"Sat sri akal, Uncleji. I need to speak to you on an urgent matter," a visibly anxious Ballu said.

"Okay, go ahead."

"Not here, sir. Can we go to your office for a few minutes?"

I looked at my watch and said, "Ballu, I must leave immediately. I'm getting late."

"Uncle ji...'.

"I'll see you later in the day."

I noticed disappointment on the youngster's face.

* * *

On the way, I felt sorry for Ballu. I could not have explained to him how important my work in the police lines was. I could make out from his body language that his own concern was uppermost in

13 Police lines is where the personnel of the armed reserve available with a district are stationed, typically at the district headquarters. The arms and ammunition are also stored here.

his mind. I was prioritising the interrogation of someone who could give us vital clues to locate Jassi.

During our search for Jassi, SHO Bhola Singh of the Bilsanda police station came across Jassi's friend, Narendar aka Nanhe. In the preliminary questioning carried out by Bhola Singh, it turned out that Nanhe was in awe of Jassi, whom he called 'Jasvinder boss'. The honorific 'boss' was his acknowledgement of Jassi being superior to him and the use of Jassi's full name was to further establish the elevated station to which he was deemed to belong.

I decided to grill Nanhe in a room which stood at the corner of the police lines campus. The room was once a stable and had remained empty since the replacement of horses with two-wheeler and four-wheeler machines. However, it was still called the *astabal*.

When I told Bhola Singh to get Nanhe to the *astabal,* he smiled. He knew the meaning of such an order. This was a room which was maintained almost like a museum. None of the fixtures had been removed. The stalls, which were four in number, were still there. To add to the authenticity of the ambience, there were some saddles and harnesses placed dramatically. Horse shoes were nailed to the walls with the names of the horses that had worn them. In some cases, there were descriptions underneath of the successes that had been achieved when they were used for chasing criminals trying to evade the pursuing police officers. There were also ominous-looking wrought iron rings fastened to the walls, which were meant for tying up the misbehaved and frisky horses. To add to the drama, there were equestrian whips, crops and ring snaffle bits, some of which were kept in a polished condition. There were stories that went around in the town about the methods that were used for the interrogations that were conducted in this room – mostly exaggerated, though some were not entirely untrue.

My favourite prop among the ones on show was the ring snaffle bit, which is the most common type of bit used while riding horses. It consists of a bit mouthpiece with a ring on each side and acts through the direct pressure applied by the rider. The bit is placed across the mouth of the horse, while the rings on either side are pulled by the reins to control the direction and speed of the horse. I find it a cruel device which must be very irksome and at times, painful to the horse, although I understand its utility for the rider. Why was it my favourite prop? Simply because it created a fear in the mind of the person being interrogated that he may have to face the fate of a horse.

The equestrian whips and sticks are used to discipline horses should they be naughty or at other times, for giving them the necessary message when jumps are to be negotiated. Although, these sticks are picked up by the investigator early in the process of coercing the suspect to reveal information, their use is mostly restricted to pose a threat. The bits, likewise, are never inserted into the mouth of the suspect, but their mere display usually does the trick of softening even hardened criminals.

As it often happens, if the need to introduce the bit as a device for our purpose in the *astabal* arose, the suspect was proving to be hard to crack. In such situations, the conversation amongst the interrogators would be on the following lines:

"*Daroga ji*, the time has come."

"Do you mean that he needs to be helped to open his mouth?"

"*Ji haan, ab zaroori hai.*"

"Tell me, which one will fit his mouth?"

At this point, a number of ring snaffle bits, both the ones which have been freshly polished as well as others which have years of dust on them, are placed on the table right under the face of the suspect with a resounding thud.

"Which one shall we try first?"

A particularly old bit with loads of soot on it would be dangled and a faux attempt at measuring the mouth of the suspect would be made. This repulsive action often made the suspect much weaker and substantially easier to break. Up till this point, the suspect has not been touched even once by the interrogator, yet the atmosphere in the *astabal* delivers a telling dent to his reserves.

When Nanhe was brought in, the *astabal* was in darkness. Only two ventilators at a height of about twelve feet above the ground were kept open through which a very small amount of light was trickling in as the faint January sun was setting. The floor was uneven; at places, the soft earth had been displaced by the movement of feet. So, in the semi-darkness, the suspect came in with a degree of rattled composure. Nanhe was helped by Bhola Singh to find the stool which was kept there for him.

Slowly, but surely, Nanhe started to make something out of what surrounded him. It was then that he noticed me across the table which separated his perch from my chair. He looked at me as if he had seen a ghost and let out what can only be described as a subdued shriek. He must have noticed the intensity with which my penetrating gaze was fixed on his face. It must have occurred to him at that moment that we were going to ferret out the truth from him.

"Nanhe, do you know where you are?"

He looked at me blankly and seemed to have lost his voice.

I repeated my question.

"*Thana*?" His answer was more like a question.

"*Astabal. Suna hai kabhi?*"

There was a look of recognition on his face immediately. I could discern an expression of fear as well. He looked around and must have been able to decipher a number of things which belong to a stable for horses. His quick look around ended at my face; apprehension was writ large on his.

"So, do you know what this room means?"

He squirmed on the stool but did not say anything.

I shifted a bit in my chair and picked up a whip which was lying a little distance away. I looked at the leather whip, smiled and then turned to Nanhe.

"Tell me."

"Sir, I will tell you whatever I know. Please don't beat me."

"Why will we beat you? If you cooperate, you don't need to be scared. If you don't, then of course, we have our methods." Saying so, I looked at the whip once again.

"What do you want to know?.'"

"Where is Jassi?"

"Sir, Jassi....?"

"*Haan,* Jassi, your Jasvinder boss."

"Sir, he does not tell me anything. He vanishes for days

together. I can only tell you two or three locations where he can be found."

I asked Bhola Singh to pass on instructions to the concerned police stations to raid the locations and see if Jassi could be found there.

I was happy that Nanhe was so forthcoming. I decided to adopt a conversational style in order to extract some more information from him.

"Why do you call him 'boss'?"

"Sir, he is so special. He is superior. He has a style, a swagger which no one else has."

"What has he achieved?"

"Sir, if you look at him, you too will be under his spell. He has charisma." He spoke as if he was talking about some demi-god.

"Answer my question. What does he do? He does not work with his father at the sweet shop. He is not working anywhere. What is the source of his income?"

"Sir, he has no set pattern. He defies all stereotypes. He is like Phantom!"

This was getting to be too much. I hit the table violently with the whip in my hand. I shouted, "Havaldar, get the black bit. *Saale ke mooh mein thoons do*!" I was losing patience. The *astabal* had become dark. I asked for all the lights to be switched on. The next moment, the room was bathed in bright light. Nanhe must have noticed that my mood was far from conciliatory.

"Look, Nanhe. We do not have the whole day to get the truth out of you. We will persist and extract the information from you.

Sooner rather than later we will run out of patience. It is your choice if you want to walk out of this *astabal* on your own feet or play I-do-not-know and crawl out of here in a shape in which your best friends will not be able to recognise you."

For effect, a couple of the bits were plonked on to the table with a jarring metallic sound. Moments later, Nanhe was talking.

"Sir, Jasvinder boss... er... I mean Jassi, gets his money by supplying drugs to some of the Sikhs who have recently come to Pilibhit from Punjab. I understand that some of these men have weapons and have come here to take shelter due to the pressure being exerted by the Punjab police."

"Well done. Continue."

"Sir, I have two names which may help you track down Jassi. One is Kuljeet aka Jeette and the other is Harjinder Singh. They are the carriers of drugs when Jassi has to make a delivery."

"Where can these two be found?"

"I can give you their addresses."

The magic of the *astabal* seldom failed.

* * *

Minutes later, Kuljeet aka Jeette, had been brought to the *astabal*. A man of average height and one who could pass off for every third Sikh in the Pilibhit countryside, Kuljeet looked sickly and bereft of energy. He looked about disinterestedly at the surroundings. It was a surprise for me because in my experience I had noticed that all those who came to this museum-like room evinced interest in all that was on display. Kuljeet seemed to have something else on his mind.

"Jeette, *tera dhandha kaisa chal raha hai*?"

There was no immediate response. After a silent minute or so, Jeette shifted in his stool and almost fell down as his balance was disturbed. He exclaimed, "*Waheguru*," in a gruff mumble. I extended a hand to help him regain his composure though he did not seem to notice.

Once he had resumed his perch, I asked once again, "Jeette, how is your business doing?"

He looked at me blankly for a moment and then responded, "Which business?"

"The business of supplies."

"Supplies... what are you talking about?"

"You know very well what I am referring to. Don't feign ignorance."

"I am jobless. There is no business."

His flat denial of the activity about which we had learned from Nanhe, made me wonder for a fleeting moment if we could rely on the latter. Yet, it was clear from our detailed interrogation that many facts that the latter had presented, made the information about Kuljeet aka Jeette and Harjinder Singh stand on firm ground. I brushed aside the momentary spell of doubt. As if to celebrate the restoration of my faith in what I had learned from Nanhe, I decided to change gears in the interrogation of Jeette. The time had come to unleash a little of what the *astabal* was known for – hard interrogation.

I asked Shivdan to work on Jeette.

The opening sentence spoken by the young deputy superintendent of police was peppered with 'highly evolved' cuss words. One thing, however, was clear. It had an immediate impact on Jeette who seemed to have woken up from a slumber. He looked wide-eyed at Shivdan who held a stick in one hand and a bit dangling in the other. His posture could be roughly described as though he was about to pounce on Jeette with the ferocity of a predator.

"So, you have forgotten what *dhandha* you do?" Saying so, he hit the table with the stick to give Jeette an idea about the likely blow that he could deliver on his body.

"Sir, I will tell you everything. Just give me some water. I am thirsty."

Water was given to him, accompanied by a stern warning delivered by Shivdan in his flowery language, "Now, you will get water only after all answers have been given by you." Saying so, he pointed to a rusted iron ring grouted into a wall. "Do you see that ring? We tie up disobedient horses there. Even asses!" He let out a loud laugh at his own joke.

"Sir, I will answer whatever you ask me."

"First of all, answer what Kaptan sahib was asking you. What dhandha do you do? *Kharcha-paani kahan se aataa hai*?"

"Sir, I am a poor man. I am a farm labourer and do not even earn enough to feed myself."

"Really? What do you do with the money you get from supplying drugs?"

This was an invitation for Shivdan to deliver a series of resounding slaps on the cheeks of Jeette. He then picked up the stick again and gave a couple of blows on his legs, making Jeette howl loudly.

"Sir, yes, I supply drugs."

"We know that, of course. Tell us the names of those who receive these supplies."

"I deliver them but do not know the names of those who consume them."

"Tell us the addresses where you deliver."

He named Harjinder. This confirmed what Nanhe had told us. Armed with the addresses and leads we could dig out of Jeette, we were on our way to get Jasvinder.

* * *

Gangs

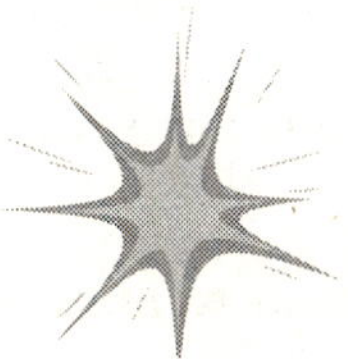

A number of search parties worked through an entire night of that Terai winter. It was biting cold, with the temperature close to freezing point. Most of our parties were moving about on motorcycles and the jeeps that some had the facility to use, were seen as a luxury. One village to another, hamlet after hamlet, *jhalas* and more *jhalas* - the search went on, seemingly endlessly. It was finally in the early hours of the morning that our radio communication broke the news for which all of us had been waiting. Our hard work finally bore fruit.

There was a message from Naresh Singh, SHO, Madhotanda station, just as I had gobbled up a quick breakfast: "Sir, we have learned about a godown which has been hired by one Rajvir in the Madhotanda area. I have pinpointed information that this name is an alias for Jassi. A raid there would bear useful results." I could not have asked for a better topping for my meal.

"What are the chances of resistance there? Do you expect to run into some armed men? I am keen to take action immediately," I said with a degree of excitement.

"Sir, I have been told that Jassi likes to keep this place out of bounds for everyone, except those who have a specific reason to be there. I am told that he may be hibernating these days because most of the buyers of his musical instruments are observing an off-season spell."

"Anyway, keep sufficient force ready. I will soon join you to carry out a raid."

It took less than an hour to reach Madhotanda. From there, we went to the village Anandpur aka Bhagwantpur. We had a section and a half (about fifteen men) of well-armed PAC men. I had a gunner with me and the SHO had two men with him who were armed with AK-47 rifles. Before leaving for our destination, the party was briefed in detail. On our way to Jassi's godown, we picked up Naresh Singh's informer to guide us to the exact spot.

The shed pointed out to us by the informer hardly looked like a place which could be associated with the savagery that one would expect in a hideout of militants. I found the surroundings somewhat underwhelming. They were far from the nearest cluster of human dwellings and gave the impression that the tip-off was inaccurate. The informer, however, was confident. Based on his input, we surrounded the shed from all sides. Two teams of two men each were ready with grenades to deal with the situation if it became necessary to storm the building. We also located an opening in the wall where two jawans were stationed with teargas shells to force the inmates to come outside if such a requirement arose. We took our positions with Sten guns[14] on either side of the

---

14 A family of British submachine guns.

door and a number of *jawans*, SHO Naresh Singh and I forced our way in.

Surprisingly, we found the hall which we entered to be almost completely empty. Only a few Indian musical instruments, most of which were in need of repairs, were lying in one section. There was a door at the end of the hall which was opened by a tall, dark Sikh man, almost at the moment we were about to force it open. The occupant was visibly surprised to come face-to-face with us, but managed to maintain his composure and asked, "What is all this? Why are there so many policemen here?"

I told him that he would learn the purpose of our visit in a while and asked him about the use to which the compound was being put.

He replied, "I deal in musical instruments. This is my godown to store the supplies."

I ordered that the room in which he was sitting, be thoroughly searched. The attached washroom was also combed through. Nothing incriminatory was found. I asked Naresh Singh to carry out a careful search of the area where the musical instruments were lying. I asked the Sikh man for an identification card while the search was being carried out. His name on his identity card read Jasvinder Singh. I found it strange that he had not offered me an identification card that carried the name of his alias, Rajvir.

A little later, Naresh came to me and whispered, "Sir, could you please come out for some time?"

"Sure," I said and accompanied the SHO to the stack of

instruments, where he showed me the inside of a *sitar*.[15] Inside the *tumba*, there was some sticky stuff resembling black jaggery. I could recognise in an instant that this was a remnant of opium which must have been transported inside the chamber. This was a clear indication that in the guise of his business, Jassi was involved in dealing with drugs.

We seized the instruments and took Jassi into custody. The entire process was carried out without a shot being fired, any force being used or harsh words spoken.

***

Jasvindar aka Jassi was our next guest in the *astabal*. His entry and manner of greeting us was underlined by a polish which surprised me.

Contrary to my expectation, Jassi actually turned out to be a mild-mannered man. A tall and dark Sikh, he had fairly handsome facial features. On closer examination, though, I found him to be shifty-eyed. He displayed all the characteristics that one would associate with a wily person. I looked at him as a person with an exterior that shrouded many untold stories involving dealings which possessed the elements of crime and other evil, yet he seemed to be remarkably cool and composed. There seemed to be many layers to his persona and that excited me as an interrogator.

I told Shivdan Singh to leave so that he may take some rest after having conducted interrogations and raids for nearly twenty-four hours. He said he was keen to interrogate Jassi.

---

15 An Indian musical instrument with two *tumbas* (hollow spherical resonating spherical chambers, the larger one of which is made of dry gourd).

"Sir, I have never interrogated such a suave suspect. This will be a new learning experience for me," he whispered in English. It was our understanding that we would use English when we wanted to avoid being understood by the person being interrogated.

I replied in the same language, keeping my volume very low, "Yes, I concur. This one seems to be urbane and cultivated. I would be keen to unravel his reality. Is he just slick or truly sophisticated?" I added, "You need to get some rest. You can go at any time of your choosing."

"But, sir, you have not rested a wink the whole day and more."

"Let us grill this savvy guy. That will be refreshing."

***

"Okay, Jassi. We will ask you some questions and want you to give us truthful answers. Is that understood?"

"Sir, I will try my best. I will share whatever knowledge I have."

"We have learned that you receive supplies of drugs from some peddlers and pass them on to your buyers. Is that true?"

"No, I have nothing to do with drug supplies."

As he said this, he gestured with his left hand to indicate that the charge was baseless. I noticed that he was wearing an expensive watch, one which would cost a couple of lakhs.

"What do you do? Are you a farmer or do you own some business?"

"I am both a farmer and have trading deals as well."

"What do you trade in?"

"I export musical instruments."

"Do you travel abroad?"

"Yes, I have travelled to Canada a number of times. I have also been to Britain and a few other European countries."

"Do you speak English?"

"I have to interact with clients. English is the most commonly used language."

Shivdan and I exchanged glances. Jassi smiled as we did that.

"What are the other languages in which you converse with your clients?"

"Mostly Punjabi."

"Do you have Punjabi clients?"

"Yes, many of them are Punjabis. They are Punjabis settled in Canada and the UK."

I told Jassi that I wanted to examine his passport. He said that it was in a hotel where he usually stayed. Shivdan accompanied him to the hotel and came back with the passport.

An examination of the passport revealed that Jassi was a frequent traveller to Canada. He had travelled to that country several times recently.

"You travel frequently to Canada. What is the business that takes you there so often?"

"I supply musical instruments. The flutes made in Pilibhit are preferred by some of our buyers."

"Is there anything else that takes you to Canada?"

"No, nothing else."

I could sense a shift of his gaze which was a giveaway.

"You are lying. What is the truth?"

Jassi shifted in his seat and once again, I discerned some signs of an effort on his part to cover up the erosion of the cockiness that he had displayed so far.

"I am waiting," I said and added, "I don't have all day."

One minute passed. He was silent. Some more time passed. Still, he made no move to talk. I felt as though he was testing my patience. Or, was it that he was thinking of what to reveal and how to keep some of the facts under wraps? I stood up and began to pace the stable. I stood in front of the wall on which a number of horseshoes were displayed with interesting descriptions associated with them. I read that one of the horses had jumped from a ten-foot high cliff while chasing a brigand and ended up fracturing its leg.

I turned to Jassi to confront him with that piece of trivia. "Do you see to what lengths we go to pursue criminals? We have many such stories in this place. We will not let you go without giving us the information for which we are looking."

"Yes, you have quite a place here. I had heard of the *astabal*, now I am seeing it."

"You have seen nothing yet. Has anyone told you why this place is so feared?"

"No, I can only guess."

"You don't have to guess. My colleague will give you the real taste of this place now."

Saying so, I nodded to Shivdan, signalling that he could take over and unleash the *astabal* magic.

I left for my residence to steal a few winks of sleep.

Back at home, I found Maanas to be still unwell and in need of immediate medical attention.

***

In the meantime, at the *astabal*, there was an exciting development. The unleashing of one trick after another had led to the complete surrender of Jassi. He broke down the moment he was threatened with the insertion of a rusted old bit into his mouth. It was accompanied by much drama and the suggestion of having the metallic bit with rings dangling on the two sides being pulled by reins. As it so often happened, this brought the shifty-eyed man to his knees, begging to be spared the torture. He promised to tell us the facts as he knew them.

Shivdan was understandably elated that the overnight *astabal* treatment had brought about the desired results. Jassi had promised to sing. Whatever he was likely to tell us would sound like sweet music.

As I entered the *astabal*, I asked Jassi if he had been extended proper hospitality in keeping with the reputation of the location. He smiled in response to my prickly question and said, "Now I know what it means to spend a night in this place." He squirmed in pain as he spoke.

"Without any preliminaries, I will come straight to the questions. Answer them honestly, else the *astabal* treatment will be repeated."

"Where do you get the money for the drugs?" I asked.

"I contribute from my own earnings, just as some others with a common cause do."

"What is the common cause?"

"We want to avenge Operation Blue Star. That's a wound that will not heal till we have our own land, Khalistan."

Having heard from him clearly that his intentions were seditious, I knew that we were dealing with a red-hot criminal.

"So, who are these soldiers of your cause who contribute money?"

"They are mostly based in Canada, but there are a couple of others too."

"How is the money collected and carried to India?"

"We have *hawala* dealings."

"Name a few *hawaladars* handling this."

"They are faceless and incognito persons. We never come to know the real people but the whole deal is based on implicit trust."

"Do you know someone called Darbara Singh?"

"Do you mean Professor Darbara Singh?"

"Yes."

"Of course, he is a scientist and an authority on modern dairy farming."

"Is he just that? Or are there other aspects to his activities?"

Jassi remained quiet for several minutes, then shook his head and said, "None that I know of."

I looked deep into his shifty eyes and that was enough to break his armour.

"Sir, he is a sympathiser. His mission is to create public awareness and spread the message of a separate land for Sikhs."

My suspicion about the professor actually being a disruptor was confirmed. I was happy that we had arrested him and that our case against him was becoming stronger with fresh evidence.

Jassi also gave us some vital clues about the drug trade across the Indo-Nepal border and the connection of this smuggling with raising funds for arms, ammunition and other logistics for the militants. He could not, however, give us any clues about the sources of the arms and ammunition that the militants were receiving. He said that no fresh supplies of arms were materialising. Ammunition, too, was in short supply.

I was convinced that the most reliable leads to locate Mark Stallion will come from Jassi. The fact that information was not just trickling from him, but had assumed the form of a robust stream, made me excited.

"Jassi, we are now close to the end of our current conversation. I expect you to understand that we have our sights fixed on certain individuals who are causing the maximum damage in my district and other parts of Terai. One of them is Mark Stallion as we call him in the police force. You, of course, know who I am talking about." I paused to see his reaction. Once again, his evasive instincts seemed to inhibit his willingness to share the information which he certainly had.

"I am waiting, Jassi. Don't make me wait too long."

Jassi's body language was now of a man who was grappling with dual threats, one from the police and the other from the source of terror. He was perceptibly weighing the relative damage either side could cause him. He had to make a quick decision then and there.

"Sir, I am not sure who you call Mark Stallion."

"Really?" I spoke in a low voice, but the aggression in my tone and the look in my eyes seemed to rattle him. To add to the effect, I picked up a stick and looked at it intently as though I was assessing its potential for breaking down Jassi.

I stood up and picked up an old horseshoe from a shelf. The label next to it read, 'Worn by Sultan, the gallant black stallion. Martyred 23 January 1934, in chasing Brigand Bhagwati successfully'.

I turned to Jassi and said to him, "Do I need to tell you that the brave fighters of crime don't fear death? Policemen are face-to-face with danger all the time." After a pause, I added, "I am willing to go to any lengths to get the truth out of you. Mind you, there will be no compromises on this. If we need to nail horseshoes onto your soles, we'll do that too!"

I resumed my seat to glare into Jassi's eyes. He had a hard time meeting my gaze.

"Jassi, don't try my patience anymore."

The next moment, Jassi mentioned the real name of the militant who we called Mark Stallion in low whispers. As he did that, he looked around lest someone spot him. I asked him to give locations where we could find him. He told us three places, two of which were the same as Darbara Singh, the 'Professor', had given us. I now had the information that one could rely on when action was to be mounted to track down Mark Stallion.

Based on other information that we could extract from Jassi, we had a list of a number of local citizens of the Pilibhit countryside who had joined the militants from Punjab. The total number of such desperados was sixty-seven, after the additions we made, based on interrogations carried out in the *astabal*. The police stations which were most affected included Gajraula, Puranpur, Madhotanda, Hazara, Neuria, Amaria and Bilsanda.

We gave names to these gangs based on the areas in which they were usually hiding and in some cases, their modus operandi. Two gangs were named after their prominent leaders. The Gajraula gang was called Lal Gajar (red carrot), the Madho Tanda gang was named Thanda Madho (cold Madho), the gang led by Karnail Singh was called the Colonel's Company, the one led by Preetam Chhina was called the Chimpanzee and the gang which had the most dangerous firepower was given the name Dhamaka (explosion) gang. Most of these gangs had accepted the dominance of Mark Stallion, whose gang had only four permanent members, all from Punjab and he would co-opt the services of other gangs, depending on the requirements of the raid he was planning.

The possession of dependable data and information is key to planning an offensive. We were now in a position to feel confident that we had the names of criminals who were required to be accounted for. The gang lists were updated with an accuracy which gave us the confidence to recognise who were the enemies.

***

Jassi came into the picture when Inder had told us about Sheru. We grilled Jassi for several hours to get facts about this enigmatic character who could be a vital link in establishing the connection between the militants who were active in Pilibhit and those in Punjab. Jassi was evasive. He denied any knowledge of Sheru altogether. We described the man and showed photographs to him to jog his memory. He continued to deny having any knowledge. Yashbir, Shivdan and I discussed the matter. Our collective conclusion was that Jassi was speaking the truth on this matter and we could keep this query on the back burner for the moment.

The formalities of presenting Jasvindar aka Jassi, Harjinder and Kuljeet aka Jeette before the Terrorist and Disruptive Activities (Prevention) Act (TADA) court were fulfilled and police custody was granted. Apart from Jassi, Nanhe was also presented before the special court trying cases of Narcotic Drugs and Psychotropic Substances (NDPS) Act for his participation in the possession and transportation of drugs. Two days later, we intercepted Harjinder while he was trying to cross the border into Nepal. He, too, was sent to judicial custody on our request. The task was cut out for our interrogators to grill them over the subsequent days.

* * *

After a long and tiring day, I was in my bed. Lying next to me was Maanas who had recovered sufficiently to sleep peacefully unlike the previous few days. Despite the need for sleep and back-breaking fatigue, I was wide awake, thinking about the dramatic revelations that had been made by the witnesses at the *astabal*.

My thoughts were centred particularly on Jassi. Nanhe had painted a larger-than-life image of him; he had called him Phantom. The awe with which he called him 'boss' was haunting me. If Jassi was actually the champion that he was made out to be, why did he spill the beans in just one session? I was also wondering about the denial he made about Sheru. How could it be that Sheru's name did not ring a bell for him? How could he be so poker-faced even when the photographs were shown to him? I decided that we should spend more time on this aspect when we got the opportunity to grill him during police custody.

I could not keep my mind at rest. I wondered whether it was safe to rely on what he had told us. Was it wise to plan our offensive based on what we had learned from him about the gangs' firepower and strength? I was tossing and turning in my bed, careful to not disturb the toddler whose expression was so completely devoid of any evil. I must have dozed off fitfully, while the thoughts of the crooked world still played in my conscience.

***

Behind Bars

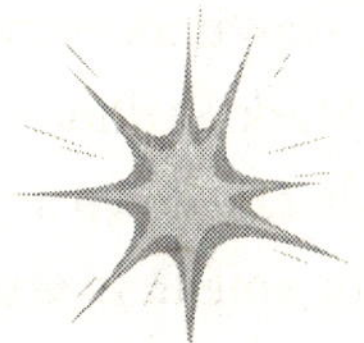

I had spent only a few weeks in Pilibhit and there was already so much action – enough for several months in most cases. A terror attack on my residence, the spotting of suspicious movement in forests around the town, an attempt to photograph my car leading to a daylight capture in the buzzing bazaar of a man in contact with militant facilitators, the identification of a financer of the desperados and also of one of their ideologues. Things were moving at a breakneck speed and I was not spending enough time with people who needed my attention to address problems.

Ballu was one such individual, a teenager who said that he did not want to share his problems with other officers. He considered his issue too important a matter to be dealt with by anyone other than the chief of the district police. I presumed that he had something important to convey to me, yet, what surrounded me was too throttling to allow me any breathing space. At the back of my mind, I knew that the oxygen which I needed to establish clarity was in meeting the people from the public.

The upshot gathered on the previous evening at the *astabal* was a case in point. Jasvinder aka Jassi had given leads, but there was a doubt which haunted me throughout the night – was Jassi so forthcoming with information with an underlying motive to derail the progress that was underway in mounting an attack on militants, especially Mark Stallion? How could such a cold-blooded scheming man break down to the extent that he did? Was there a rat I did not smell? It was dawning on me that I did not have sources of intel that could be relied upon, persons whose information was not a bitter pill dipped in sugar. I needed to get fresh inputs before the available information was put to the ultimate test – that of taking on the adversary and exposing ourselves to possible fatal losses.

I was lost in these thoughts when a constable attracted my attention due to the high volume in which he was talking to someone in the reception area of the camp office. I called him in to enquire the reason for the commotion. He was someone I had not seen before. So, I asked him who he was.

"Sir, my name is Shekhar Dabral. I have been sent for this duty to fill in for a constable who is on leave."

I started to wonder if he was speaking the truth. Such was the state of my mind. Was I becoming paranoid?

"Sir, one Sukhbir Singh Kohli wants to meet you and I told him that you have left instructions for not being disturbed. He is insisting that I tell you that he is here."

"Oh, that must be Sukhi. Let him come in."

The next moment, the cheerful visage of Sukhi lifted my spirits. He broke into an uninhibited laughter which displayed genuine happiness on seeing me. I cannot claim that I was not similarly thrilled to see him though his manner of greeting brought a certain calm to my troubled mind. As we made small talk, I started to think about the doubts I had in my mind about his true intentions. The fact that he introduced me to Professor Darbara Singh and the subsequent revelations about the old man's actual mission, had clouded my mind for some time. Now that Sukhi was before me, I somehow felt completely sanguine about his trustworthiness; he had that kind of aura about him. In the meantime, the LIU watch kept over him had also come up with a sparkling clean chit.

"Hello, Sukhi. How have you been?" I asked, though I sensed an element of reserve in my own speech.

"Good and I have something important to tell you."

"Go ahead. I am all ears, Sukhi."

"I have learned that you have entertained some important guests at the *astabal*."

I was surprised that he knew about the grilling sessions of the previous two days and nights.

He sensed my reaction and said, "When someone is investigated in depth, when there are no holds barred and the method rarely fails, the *astabal* comes into the picture. Doesn't it, Lal sahib?"

"What have you learnt, Sukhi?" I asked with a bit of apprehension.

"I have learnt that a few suspects were interrogated and you were heading the team. It was confirmed when you sought their custody for further investigation."

"Is this the talk of the town?"

"Not really. But this being a small town, it will not be long before the public comes to know."

"Do you want to tell me something about the people who were grilled?"

"Jassi was the most important catch among the ones you grilled. The others are of only limited significance. They are just being used as *coolies* according to the information I have gathered. Jassi is close to the core group of the militants and he could even be in the know of the location and plans of the top men like Mark Stallion. Therefore, I see the likelihood of rich returns if he is grilled more and with greater vigour." After a pause, he added, "He is deceptive. You cannot trust him on face value. His arrest may also have been an initiative from his side. He might be cooking something in the jail."

Sukhi looked intently at me, as though he was trying to read my reaction to what he had told me. I tried not to give myself away, even while I weighed the import of what he had said. Beady of eye and rubicund of visage, this engaging man was blooming and glowing as usual, yet, his expression wore a certain foreboding which I could not gloss over.

"Lal sahib, I hope you will plan your moves with great care. You are not dealing with novices."

"Yes, of course. I do have an idea about the gravity of the situation. The police will not make any hasty moves without first pondering over all possible aspects and consequences."

After a well-contemplated pause, I asked him, "Sukhi, do you know someone nicknamed Sheru?"

He reflected for some time and then, shook his head in the negative. After some more rumination, he asked, "Where did you hear this name? Who told you?"

"Someone mentioned this name and I thought that the walking encyclopaedia would have the answer," I smiled.

"I will make enquiries."

"Please do so, but very carefully. I don't want to alert any suspicious characters about the knowledge we have gathered."

"Yes, Lal sahib."

As he rose to leave, he said, "I have some really rare stuff to wash away all worries. Please join me this evening."

I just smiled back.

* * *

"We have to weigh all the information we have gathered in the last two or three weeks very carefully and make sense of it to frame a clear strategy to control militancy," I said, as an opening remark at a meeting with my colleagues, not long after Sukhi had left. I must say that I was a little rattled to learn that the operations being carried out by our uninvited guests were aimed at a long-drawn battle. I wanted my colleagues to be on the same page as me.

Additional SP Yashbir Bisht said, "Sir, after yesterday's revelations at the *astabal*, I think we are good to go."

"Please give the whole matter some more thought. Let us

cross-check the dependability of what we have learnt in the last two days from different sources," I interjected, by way of caution.

"Of course, I am not advocating a leap without due caution. What I mean to put across is that with what we learnt yesterday, after you took the lead in our interrogations, we should feel sufficiently confident to take on our adversaries."

"It was a team effort. We have good reason to feel satisfied with what we have achieved. However, it is always better to mount an offensive after due preparation. Being well-armed with information is one important aspect of being prepared," I said.

Yashbir nodded in agreement.

Shivdan Singh said, "Sir, I watched you yesterday and admired the manner in which you managed to prise out information. I think what we have learnt is enough to plan our moves. However, I am not sure if we have the weapons and other wherewithal to meet the challenge."

"Shivdan, I must, once again, stress upon the fact that our success yesterday was the outcome of exemplary teamwork. You played an important role. However, to be on a safe wicket, we must verify our information. As for weapons and other infrastructural requirements, it is going to take a while for the government to actually respond to our requests. First of all, it has to be acknowledged that there is actually militancy here; only then will our machinery be geared up to face this challenge. However, we cannot wait for weapons to arrive before we go into a battle which cannot be postponed. That is beyond our control. We have to fight bravely with whatever we have. Our best weapon is our own morale and our commitment to root out militancy from Pilibhit."

I turned to inspector LIU and gave him instructions to gather intelligence to cross-check what we had learned from Jassi. I also asked him to closely examine the entire route that Professor Darbara Singh had followed and prepare a detailed report about the persons he had met. The circle officers and SHOs were told to alert their sources. I emphasised repeatedly that our best weapon was information - the more accurate it was, the more assured we would be of success.

"During the period of custody, I would like to form two teams of interrogators. One will concentrate on Darbara Singh, Kuljeet Singh and Jassi while the other will interrogate Nanhe and Harjinder. The two teams will then exchange notes to arrive at greater clarity. If needed, we will swap places to interrogate the other set of the accused," I instructed my colleagues.

* * *

I asked Shivdan to stay after the meeting was over.

"Shivdan, you were instrumental in breaking Jassi. He gave enough information for us to think in terms of planning our operations on an aggressive scale. What is your personal take on his revelations? Please give a frank opinion. You need not hold back anything."

He thought for a while before saying, "We should be very happy with what we got from him. It is not often that one gets to interrogate someone who appears to be a part of the core team of militants. Sir, we should value the information for another reason – such an arrest is not an everyday happening and people like Jassi do not easily reveal so much."

"Yes, Shivdan, I agree that these hardened criminals who are driven by the desire to accomplish what they consider a mission are hard nuts to crack. It is in this context that I want you to tell me if Jassi did not break too easily?"

Shivdan was silent for some time and then nodded his head in affirmation of what I had said.

"So, you also feel that we might have been fed misinformation to derail our progress?"

"Yes sir, we cannot rule out that possibility."

We were in contemplation for several minutes when all of a sudden, we both spoke at the same time.

"Listen, Shivdan..."

"Sir, I have an idea..."

"Okay, go ahead, Shivdan."

"Sir, I'm sorry for the interruption. You first, please."

"No Shivdan, let me hear what you have to say first."[16]

"Right, sir. I think we should send someone into the jail and eavesdrop on what these criminals are discussing with each other. I think it will be possible to stage an arrest of our own informer."

"That's a brilliant idea, Shivdan. There is, however, a catch. The likes of Jassi and Darbara are going to be very careful and will not make any plans when others can get a whiff of what is

16 About a decade later, I received a call from Shivdan. He was SP in a district in UP. He recalled this conversation and told me that it was a learning moment for him. He understood the importance of listening to opinions even if they came from lower ranks. He said that he had also gathered that if the boss has an opinion, it should only be expressed after he has heard from others, otherwise a frank exchange of ideas would not take place.

being discussed. Our informer will also be exposed and may come to harm."

"That's right, sir."

"We know that Nanhe and Harjinder have not been charged under TADA. They are accused of narcotics offences. They have been used as conduits and there is no indication of their involvement in militant activities. I think we can hatch a deal with them."

"A deal? What sort of deal, sir?"

"Let us tell them that we will help them by being soft in opposing their applications for bail. If they take this bait, we can use them as our informers. What do you say?"

"That sounds like a great deal to me. If I were Nanhe or Harjinder, I would grab it with both hands. Jassi has been dealing with them and is not likely to doubt their intentions, even if they are around when the plans are drawn."

"Start working on this idea. Send someone in whom you have absolute confidence to the jail to meet Nanhe and Harjinder to negotiate this deal."

"Yes, sir."

* * *

What we gained from behind the walls of the district jail was game-changing. The informants, who had taken the brave step of crossing the floor – and in the process, ditching their unscrupulous exploiters – proved to be just the addition to our team that we needed in order to give ourselves the sharpness which we lacked in terms of intel.

Our brief for Nanhe and Harjinder was two-fold – one, to cross-check the information gathered at the *astabal* during the interrogation of Jassi and two, to get whatever useful information they could access while they had the opportunity to spy on Jassi and Darbara.

When stated in these simple terms, the two tasks look like a cakewalk, but they were life-threatening ventures. Our informants were powerless compared to the subjects of scrutiny they were up against – the ruthless czars of the underbelly. It was a challenge which our two fresh recruits accepted because they were in thick soup themselves, one that was largely cooked by the ones on whom they were asked to spy. Their initial response to the deal offered to them was that on one side, it is a ditch, on the other, a trench that is even deeper. They weighed a few years of incarceration against a near certain death at the hands of the militants. Their fear could not be questioned for its soundness. Indeed, it was clear what the militants' action would be. It took more than just the promise to let bail be granted to them without any opposition from our side. I must say, Shivdan's choice was astute; his asset had his way with the reluctant duo of Nanhe and Harjinder.[17]

What we gathered through Nanhe and Harjinder were sensational disclosures. There was a plan to loot three banks located in the semi-urban centres of the district, about ten persons were part of a hit list on the suspicion of being informers of the police

---

17 In the interest of keeping it confidential, the actual 'deal' is not being exposed here. The wise one said, 'some things are more eloquent when not spelled out.'

and the recruitment of young men for joining the gangs engaged in militancy was also a part of the plan.

The indication was that banks located in Puranpur, Hazara and Amaria were under threat. These banks were ones which had a relatively large transaction of cash every day. The other factor was the weak security arrangements in two of these branches. There was a police guard in the one at Puranpur, but it was ill-equipped to deal with a strong raid by the marauders. The weapons were no match for the AK rifles that the militants were likely to employ and the training that had been imparted to the men was not of the standard that was required in dealing with well-armed, hardened criminals.

We had an unconfirmed tally of about a dozen families that had found their way to a hit list drawn by the militants. We called the concerned SHOs for a meeting to understand from them the local factors of their areas that could be responsible for these names being chosen. In no less than ten cases, we found the names of such citizens who were generally of assistance to the police. In fact, in three of the cases, we could identify the specific reasons why these conscientious citizens were finding themselves on the receiving end of the militant stick.

The drive to enlist youngsters to shore up the number of active militants in order to enhance their presence and cover a wider area of influence was a headache which would be mild to begin with but threatened to assume throbbing proportions in the times to come. The seriousness of this development could not have been overstated. We could have downplayed our trepidation only to amplify the peril. Dealing with a larger number was just one of the problems; these young men had the advantage of knowing the area like the back of their hand. Their ability to make their presence felt to a frustrated police force by committing a crime and then vanishing into thin air was a possibility with which we were likely to grapple. As it is, the given number of trouble-makers was a stiff challenge; an enlarged size was an even more troubling possibility.

* * *

The Counter-Narrative

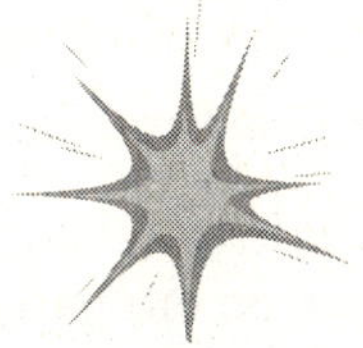

The information received by the SHO Amaria on Wednesday, 23 January, was a confirmation about the likelihood of attacks on banks. He confirmed that his sources had brought him pin-pointed intel and within the week, there was a likelihood of a strike on a branch of a bank, either in Amaria or Madhotanda. There were four open days left for the banks in the week, including Wednesday, the day we received the intelligence. It was essential to make arrangements post haste, there being the possibility of a strike by the militants as early as the same day.

It was certain that the attack would be during the working hours. Banks are mostly looted when the branch is open and the marauders have the confidence that they can overpower the bank personnel and security men, if there are any. As it turned out, both the branches did not have a security guard. There were no security cameras either.

We took the bank employees into confidence. Once they learnt about the imminent attack, most of them understandably developed a high degree of fear. In fact, they put forth the idea that the branches could remain closed during the week. Obviously, such a move was not acceptable. The state could not have been seen capitulating before a handful of criminals. That would have sent a message to the general public that the militants were reigning supreme and that the police force had surrendered. The morale of the force would have nose-dived and the public would have lost all confidence in the keepers of law.

It took much persuasion on our part to secure the presence of the managers and their skeletal staff. We allowed confirmed heart patients and others with serious comorbidities among the staff to be given leave. It was heartening to see that there were some amongst the bank employees who showed keenness to report for duty. Some of them had interesting suggestions to offer regarding dealing with the attackers, mostly based on what they had seen in films. Their lack of differentiation between real and reel was almost endearing.

We formed four teams, one for each of the branches located in Puranpur, Hazara, Amaria and Madhotanda. Each of these men was teamed up with the staff available at the banks. The idea was to make our men pose as managers, tellers and other bank employees. Each of our men was armed. Cut-off parties were posted outside the branches on nearby buildings and other vantage points. Our plan was to let the militants enter the branch and then deal with them there. This plan was necessary despite its inherent dangers. We could have missed them if we tried to deal with them before they entered the premises. There was a chance that they could escape in such a situation. Undoubtedly, it called for a great amount of courage to deal with armed criminals in a situation where there was a possibility of man-to-man scuffles and exchange of fire. Had the militants taken the initial advantage, it would have been nearly impossible to reverse the trend. Despite all these factors, the men were pumped up and optimistic about the outcome.

At about 11 a.m., the expected raid happened at Amaria. There were no customers at the branch and our staff had mingled with the bank staff quite unnoticeably. A tall turbaned man entered the branch with what appeared to be a rifle hidden under a blanket. His face was covered with one end of the turban. I was sitting in the cabin which was meant for the manager. The SHO Amaria was sitting at the far end. As soon as he noticed the man who had entered, he opened fire with his revolver. The man immediately fired back with his rifle, but by then, we had all taken our positions in relative safety behind the counters. We returned the fire and the militant understood that he was outnumbered. He fired a few more shots and then beat a hasty retreat.

As he went outside the branch, all of us cautiously made our way to the point from where the militant had entered. While we were doing this, we heard a number of gunshots from outside. As we emerged outside the branch, we found that our men atop the buildings in front were pointing towards one side and firing. We climbed into our vehicles to move in that direction. One of the men ran up to my car and informed me that the militant who had entered the branch had received a shot and was bleeding from his shoulder. The others had helped him escape with them. There was a point in this chase when we realized that the criminals had taken advantage of a jungle not far from the township and taken cover. We organized ourselves to fan out into the jungle in order to comb it. We also alerted the other three branches to be prepared for an attack from the frustrated outlaws. Our search for the militants lasted a couple of hours. We left some armed staff at the branch in Amaria and decided to visit the other branches immediately to boost their morale. The additional SP and deputy SP were sent to two branches and I went to the third one. A message was radioed to all police stations to be on the lookout for the criminals who had made the daring daylight attempt to loot the bank. It was mentioned that one of them was injured and bleeding. The whole day was spent looking for the fleeing militants. We assessed that they were five or six in number. At least twc of them were armed with rifles. The others seemed to have less sophisticated weapons.

It was disappointing for us that we had come so close to our targets and yet remained so far from them. In a debrief meeting, the point was raised that we had opened fire in the bank earlier than we should have. Had we waited a little more, maybe more criminals would have been in our range of fire. I was of the view that to allow more men to enter, armed as they were, could have proved to be fatal.

I saw something positive in what had happened. Not only was a clear signal sent to the militants that we were a step ahead of them and knew about their movements, but also, the public would see our intent and readiness to deal with hardened criminals. This was good from the point of view of keeping public morale high. Of course, the men were also ready to deal with any such situations that may precipitate in the future.

As we were about to disperse, there was a radio message from our outpost on National Highway (NH) 30 that suspicious movement had been noticed in the forest close to Jithania, located about twelve kilometres due north from where we were situated. The message also pointed to the likelihood of one of the militants being injured in one of his arms. This gave us the sense that it was the same group which had raided the bank branch in Amaria.

From a study of the map and the input provided by the policemen posted in Amaria police station, we found that we could approach the location from three directions. From the north-west, we could advance from Balliya and from the south, we had access by taking the Lahaurganj-Bilaspur-Hyderabad route on NH30. The third approach was from the east via Deorania. Three teams were formed, each led by a senior officer and at least eight armed officers and men were placed at their disposal. The SHO Amaria was asked to proceed separately and alert his informers as well as helpers from among the public. He was also given the vital duty of coordinating the movements of the three teams because his knowledge of the area was the most intimate. Each of these four parties had one AK-47 rifle each apart from other weapons. Even the availability of one powerful weapon suffused the teams with enhanced morale and confidence.

We had a quick chat among ourselves – a huddle before embarking on something that might turn out to be a big victory or the other extreme of disappointment and even loss of lives, which could not have been ruled out. I insisted that we had a clear strategy and morale on our side and that we were carrying out the pious work of fighting evil and protecting good. We had every reason to embark upon this mission with the absolute confidence that we would be victorious. What I said was imbued with the do or die emotion with an emphatic message that it was our day and we had every reason to feel assured that we will achieve the desired results.

***

My gunner, Head Constable Alimuddin, had intimate knowledge of the area we were traversing on our way to Deorania. He knew routes which were not known to others in the team that I was heading. Apart from Alimuddin and the driver, I had with me in my car Sub-Inspector Ram Darshan Yadav, the officer who covered this beat. He, too, was quite familiar with the topography and prominent residents of the region. So, my team had two highly dependable navigators. Our car was followed by a jeep carrying five men with weapons, including an AK-47. The other two teams also had a couple of vehicles each with similar firepower.

On the way, SI Ram Darshan Yadav stopped at village Rasula to make enquiries if any movement of the militants had been noticed. He came back with the information that some unknown people had actually been seen by a young boy, who had also noticed that one of them was moving with difficulty and leaning on others. So, we got confirmation that the militants had actually escaped into this area. The boy had seen them enter the jungle to the west. I alerted the other three parties on the wireless sets and advised them to be ready to deal with the desperados.

After driving to the eastern edge of the jungle, we left our vehicles and entered the woods on foot. Our movement was slow because we had to be very careful about not exposing ourselves. There were dry leaves everywhere which made crackling sounds as we stepped on them. This, we knew, was a perilous giveaway. In a situation like that, the only option was to take the unavoidable risk and draw comfort from the fact that even the adversary was dealing with the same handicap.

We had moved about half a kilometre into the jungle when there was a burst of rifle fire. One could discern that automatic rapid fire weapons were in operation. Clearly, one of the other parties had engaged the brigands in an exchange. We moved in the direction from where the shots were being heard. We had barely moved a few metres when we noticed a man running towards the north and firing intermittently with a rifle. He was unaware that in doing so, he had exposed himself to our party. We immediately took positions behind tree trunks and fired at the fleeing man. He realized that in his effort to run away from one party, he had run into another. He tried to change the direction in which he was running; in doing so, he tripped over an exposed root of a tree and fell down. As he tumbled, his weapon fell out of his hand. All of us rushed in his direction as he tried to stand up. He did not succeed in his effort and fell down once again. By then, we reached and overpowered him. Having fallen face down into the mud, it was hard to recognise him as his face was completely smeared with dirt. I asked two armed constables to tie up the man's feet and hands and keep a close watch over him. I instructed them in a loud voice, "Kill the bastard if he tries to escape."

The exchange of fire was continuing towards the western and north-western sides of the jungle. We decided to move in that direction. When we caught up with another team, we learned that the militants had run away from the spot and another party was in pursuit. The sound of firing had also stopped. I instructed this team to accompany me, except for two officers who were sent to the location where we had arrested the militant, to make sure that he was not allowed to make a getaway.

The pursuit of the rest of the gangsters continued for several hours. When it started to become dark, I decided to return to the place of arrest of the lone militant.

By the time we reached there, the face of the militant had been cleaned and I shouted in great excitement, "Sheru!"

* * *

Taming the Lion

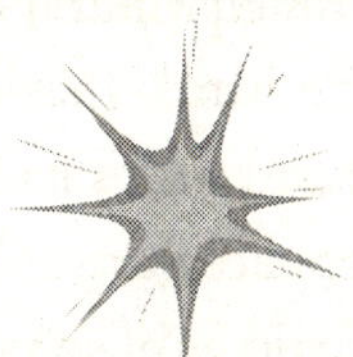

The parties who were chasing the other militants gave up the chase around midnight. Two members of the team led by Additional SP Yashbir Bisht which operated in the Lahaurganj-Bilaspur-Hyderabad area were injured during the exchange of fire. Head Constable Jagtap Singh and Constable Matru Lal received gunshot injuries; the former in the right leg above the knee and the latter in the upper left arm. They were rushed to the nearest primary health centre. After receiving the necessary first aid, both were referred to the district hospital for further treatment.

A surprise was awaiting me when I returned to the place where Sheru was in our captivity. I found Roshan Singh with the policemen there. Yes, Havaldar Roshan Singh of the CRPF, my saviour, was there! I was surprised to find him in the thick of action. My immediate reaction was to express my displeasure at his presence when I had told him very clearly that he could not participate in our operations. I was, however, softened by the memory of what he had done for me in the face of extreme adversity, a real threat to my life.

"Roshan, why are you here? With whose permission have you come here? I told you clearly that the service rules of the CRPF do not allow your participation in our operations."

"Sir, I was passing through Amaria on NH30 when I learned about the shootout at the bank. The locals told me about the direction in which the police parties had gone. They also told me that you were leading the police party. I heard an exchange of fire and came here to see if I could be of some help. Sir, tell me if there is anything that I can do for the police."

"Roshan, you are a brave and kind person. You have saved my life once, for which, I cannot express in words, the sense of gratitude I have. However, I cannot allow you to participate in our operations. As a local resident of this district, please help the police in tracking down militants and other criminals, but you have to understand the limits that bind you. I will definitely contact you, if and when I need your assistance. Thank you, my friend," I said, with a sense of sadness.

"As you order, sir! I am at your disposal. Please call me whenever you need me."

"Roshan, tell me, what is the latest news about you joining your duties?"

"Sir, I have been cleared by the team of doctors. Next month, I will go back to my battalion." He saluted smartly and left.

The day's work had brought with it a handsome reward – we had Sheru in our custody. However, the fleeing gangsters could not have been allowed to get away. I directed the SHO Amaria to continue patrolling his area and gather whatever information he could.

We took Sheru to the police station and started his interrogation. I must say that despite the vulnerable condition in which he was, he had a certain swagger in his manner. Shivdan Singh was with me and his suggestion was to put a bullet through the smug gangster's brain. A couple of other officers also nodded in agreement.

I said to Sheru, "Have you heard what they are saying? I am sure you deserve to be butchered but you do not deserve to be given such a quick death. You ought to be tortured so brutally that you yourself beg to be killed."

Sheru remained impassive and it seemed that he was ready to be tortured or even be eliminated. I asked the men to thoroughly search him in order to ascertain that he was not carrying anything that could be used for killing himself or causing harm to anyone of the police party. The search revealed that his right shoulder was wrapped in a cloth because there was a gunshot wound. So, it was Sheru who had entered the bank ahead of the rest of the gang and was shot.

"Look Sheru, your game is up. The rest of your friends are also in our custody," I lied. "It's only a matter of minutes before we get all the information for which we are looking. Let us start with you. I assure you, if you cooperate, we will not kill you."

To my surprise, Sheru nodded to indicate that he was willing to talk. He asked for water. I promised to serve it to him, provided he gave us all the information which we were seeking. He nodded yet again to convey his willingness to talk.

I asked a constable to bring water for Sheru. A little amount of the liquid was poured in a glass and placed in front of him. He picked up the glass with his left hand and gulped down the water. He looked imploringly at the constable standing with a bottle of water, who looked at me to seek my approval. I spoke in a low voice to Sheru, "Listen, I will get you not only more water, but some tea as well. Just tell me the whole plan which you were going to carry out."

Sheru did not speak for a few minutes. Ram Darshan Yadav became restive and gave Sheru a resounding slap on his cheek, enough to make him lose his balance and fall down on the ground. The once dandy gangster looked like a sorry shadow of the image that he tried to project in the photographs which we had retrieved from the camera of the owner of the photo studio, Inder. I could not help but feel sorry for him, though my abhorrence for what he was doing and the methods he employed was indelible. A young man who should be engaged in constructive pursuits had become a misguided pawn in the hands of scheming enemies of the country. How I wished that he could be retrieved from that hell and brought back into the mainstream of society and the nation!

After reflecting for a minute or two, I brought my focus back to the task at hand, which was forcing Sheru to give us information. I knew that Sheru was not likely to roar, but if he could just somehow, give us the information that we were so keen to hear. I wanted him to tell me the whereabouts of Mark Stallion and his potential targets. Only one meaningful whisper would have done the job.

It took us a gruelling twelve-hour session to make Sheru sing, but he did. We had all that we sought on Mark Stallion and more!

I spoke to District Magistrate Sharda Prasad and requested him to direct the jail authorities to keep Sheru in a solitary cell and not let him interact with visitors and other inmates, particularly the ones who were there for participation in militant activities.

***

The following morning, the senior officers were closeted with me in my private office. In this session that was devoted to a SWOT[18] analysis, we discussed the import of the revelations made by Sheru and weighed them against available information. The process was frantic owing to the importance that Mark Stallion enjoyed in terms of his notoriety in the eyes of the police force, the public at large and the awe that he inspired even in the top leadership of the K-cause. Since I was conducting the deliberations at this meeting, my job was two-fold – to keep the evaluation of our strengths at a realistic level and to assess the opponent's weaknesses on which we could capitalize.

During this discussion, I offered an appraisal of our strength, based largely on our high moral position – we were fighting evil and protecting the good and our efforts were to provide security to the peace-loving loyal citizens of the country. I realized that our weaknesses were the lack of force, insufficient number of powerful weapons and inadequate training as well as experience in dealing with violent militants. We had been offered an opportunity to score because we had reliable intelligence. We could not, however,

---

18 An acronym for strengths, weaknesses, opportunities and threats; SWOT analysis is a framework for identifying and analysing an organization's strengths, weaknesses, opportunities and threats.

overlook the threat of the opponent's methods of brutal and unscrupulous violence, helped by strong firepower. For us, it was a do or die situation and the cause was pious as well as just. Given these parameters, we concluded that we had the upper hand.

We got down to brass tacks and formed teams. Each was to be led by senior officers. One team was dedicated to all-round intelligence gathering because we needed minute-by-minute updates. Another team of officers local to the area where Mark Stallion was reportedly camping was formed under the leadership of the additional SP and included three of our best SHOs as well. This team was provided with two platoons of the Provincial Armed Constabulary, armed with self-loading rifles (SLRs). Another team, led by Shivdan Singh, was also complemented by a well-armed platoon made up of the PAC and district armed reserve. The third team was under my leadership. I had one platoon with me and two sharpshooters from among the best we boasted. All details of available vehicles, wireless communication hardware and reserve force were compiled. We dispersed around midnight. We were physically tired but our morale was high and my personal judgement of our readiness made me calm.

The next day, the operation was to start before sunrise. Sleep was nowhere in sight.

* * *

While I was trying to steal a few winks, Maanas and Madhu were both enjoying a sound sleep.

Someone knocked softly on the door. I was surprised that there was someone at the door at such an odd hour. I opened the door to find an orderly standing there with an expression I could not decipher immediately. Before I could say anything, he gave me a sealed envelope and quickly turned around to go away. Did I hear him cry?

I opened the envelope. The wireless message marked 'SECRET' had a text of just one sentence. It was my transfer order. I was required to hand over the charge to my successor a few hours later.

Madhu was woken up by the slight noise I must have made when I received the envelope. "What is it, Aloke?" She enquired.

"I'll tell you in the morning."

"I am curious. I want to know."

"I have been transferred," was my short response.

"What, transferred? But we have just come here. I have completed the unpacking of our luggage only today...," she started to sob.

I did not want to add to her misery by telling her what I was going to miss.

* * *

'Instant Justice'

13 July 1991, was the second Saturday of the month, which is observed as a holiday. I was at home in Moradabad and in the frame of mind to chill completely. I wanted to spend some quality time with Madhu and Maanas over the weekend. I told my orderly not to connect me to telephone calls without asking me about my willingness to have a conversation with the caller. This was unlike me. I advocate availability but was doing just the opposite. I was conscious of my fault. I had ignored a couple of the buzzer sounds and felt irked about being disturbed repeatedly.

The orderly sounded the buzzer yet again. The sound of telephone buzzers in the 1990s was vexing, something that seemed like a harbinger of some unpleasant news. Maybe, this was merely owing to my individual opinion or just a state of lethargic repose. I decided to receive the call in preference to another buzzer sound.

"Yes, Imran, what is it now?" I asked the orderly with some irritation.

"Sir, Havaldar Roshan Singh of the CRPF wants to speak to you. He says it is urgent. I told him..."

"Okay, connect me to him," I responded eagerly.

"Hello, Roshan. I'm so glad you have called. How are you?"

"Jai Hind, sir. I am doing well, thank you. I am in Pilibhit these days."

"*Achcha*, you must be enjoying your leave."

"Sir, have you heard about what has happened here?"

"What has happened?"

"There has been an encounter. Ten Sikhs have been killed."

"Really? Is Mark Stallion one of them?"

"Unfortunately, it is all very fishy. People are saying all kinds of things."

"What are people saying?"

"Sir, journalists are saying that the encounter is fake. The local population is also questioning it, particularly the Sikhs."

"What do you know about it?"

"Sir, the police say that there was a tip-off about some suspicious characters travelling in a bus which was on its way to Pilibhit on 12 July, when a police team stopped it at Kachla Ghat in district Badaun."

"Roshan, that's confusing. Where was this bus coming from?"

"Sir, the police version is that there were militants travelling in the guise of pilgrims. They were brought to Pilibhit yesterday and there was an encounter when the miscreants tried to escape." After a pause, he added, "Maybe it's too early to comment. But I am not convinced by the story of the police."

"Have you learned anything else?"

"Nothing more, sir. I'll call again when I have some more information."

I found that there were a lot of unanswered questions about which I wanted clarity. I called Sukhi to get his input.

"Sukhi, tell me about the encounter."

"Encounter? Lal sahib, it is all a made-up story. God will never forgive these police officers for the carnage."

"But the police say there was a tip off..."

Sukhi did not wait for me to complete my sentence and shot back, "Tip off? I know that the bus was carrying pilgrims coming all the way from far-off states like Maharashtra, MP and UP. Such pilgrim tours are not uncommon. Your time here was short, but you were going about systematically to identify militants and deal with them suitably. Now, everyone is trying to please your successor. I'm sure this drama has been staged to please him." He sounded angry, which was so different from what I had seen of him.

"How are you sure that the tip off was not right and that the travellers had the pious intention of visiting places of pilgrimage?"

"Lal sahib, I hope you are not defending this heinous act. There was no justification in pulling those poor men outside the bus and killing them without a proper inquiry. They were at least entitled to defend themselves."

"Sukhi, I can understand your indignation. You know me much better than to think that I will support a fake encounter. But the facts will emerge from a proper inquiry. Let us wait till then."

"No, there is no doubt. The inquiries will only try to whitewash the incident and cover up. My Sikh friends are angry."

I could understand Sukhi's distress. He made a valid point when he spoke of official inquiries being shams. I could not have said it to him, but my impression was the same. The tendency to cover up culpability was a common happening.

I asked the SHO of the railway police station at Moradabad to find out if the newspapers had carried any news about the Pilibhit encounter. He informed me that there was only a short clipping that spoke of encounters at three locations in which ten militants were said to have been killed by the Pilibhit police.

It was on the following day that some details were mentioned in the daily *Amar Ujala*. I knew Vishwamitra Tandon who reported for this Hindi newspaper. I contacted him on the phone. He was forthright in his response, "I was not convinced by the version of the police, so I dug deeper in order to find the real facts of the three fake police encounters and the fourth one, which to date, has not been officially admitted."

I said, "You are already calling the encounters fake. Isn't it too early to conclude that?"

His immediate reply was, "I have covered Pilibhit for a long time. Hardly anything escapes my notice. In this matter, I received the information on the morning of 13 July. My source in Madhotanda, Islamuddin Khan, rushed to my house with the information that the police had killed several Sikh youths in a fake encounter. A little later, I was told that SP Pilibhit had called a press conference at 11 a.m. I attended the meeting."

"What was the version of the police?"

"The SP was all praise for the work done and appeared to be very proud."

"Did you find any doubtful elements in the version that the SP gave?"

"I was not convinced. When I returned from the press briefing, Islamuddin was still waiting for me in my office. By then, another source had informed me that a Sikh family from Amaria, who was travelling in the same bus, had been off-loaded and sent home. They were said to be witnesses to the entire sequence of events."

"Did you get any useful information from them?"

"Unfortunately, they told me nothing. I went with Islamuddin to the village and found the family engaged in work at their farm. We asked them about the incident. They said that nothing of the kind we had heard had happened. I could make out that this denial was made due to the terror of the police. We were driving back when a Sikh youth stopped us. He told us that one of the slain teenagers was dragged out of the bus and ignoring his mother's protests, he was taken away by the police. He said that she would tell us the truth as she now had nothing to lose."

"Did you go to the teenager's mother?"

"Yes. That proved to be a big break. We reached Pistaur village where we met the mother, Jogishwar Kaur, who was sitting on a charpoy looking devastated. I could see that her eyes were red and swollen from crying. She said that the family from Amaria whom we had visited earlier was a witness to the incident and that they may not have spoken to us due to fear of the police. We drove back to Amaria. The witnesses agreed to tell us all that they knew. It was confirmed that the Sikh youths were off-loaded by policemen, their hands tied with their turbans, forced into a police van and driven away. We learned that they were later killed deep in the jungles." Vishwamitra sounded confident about his findings.

I was shaken to my core and at a loss for words.

Vishwamitra confirmed that Mark Stallion was still at large. I could not help my mind from going back to the day when we were within breathing distance of laying our hands on this prize catch. Hours before departing from Pilibhit, I was zeroing in on the 'general'. Yet now, a few months later, he was still leading his 'army'.

I was devastated. All the painstaking work put in by SP Srivastava and I had come to nought and much worse, we had to contend with the loss of innocent lives. The cover of the police had been blown and it could be years before another opportunity to corner Stallion would emerge. The faith which I had worked hard to build in the Sikh community of Pilibhit had been eroded, perhaps forever.

***

The story appeared the next day in *Amar Ujala* with the headline – 'My Son Was Killed in a Fake Encounter'.

I read the news with bated breath and closely examined the names of those who had been killed. One of the names in that list was Balvinder Singh, resident of village Pistaur.

My heart sank. Ballu was gone!

A deep sense of guilt engulfed me. Ballu had come to meet me more than once, but I had prioritised my other work over what he wanted to tell me. More than three decades have passed and I have tried to rationalise my response. However, the nightmare with which this book opens keeps coming back to me. Maybe I am subconsciously still wandering the lanes of the nondescript villages of Terai in my search for Ballu's house. I wake up from these nightmares with a shock, look all around to find myself on my own bed with one question haunting me:

"Sardarji, where is Balvinder Singh's home?"

* * *

Epilogue

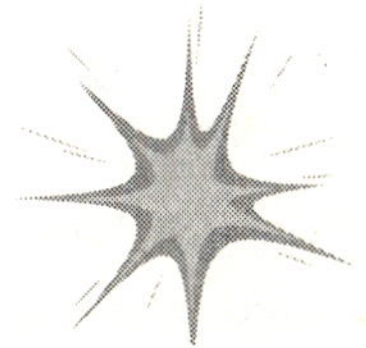

In the tragic Pilibhit encounter killings of 12/13 July 1991, the CBI concluded that the police party had committed a massacre. The prayer was for capital punishment. The CBI Special Court awarded life imprisonment to 47 police officers and men on 4 April 2016, almost twenty-five years after the carnage. Ten of the charge-sheeted police officials died during the period of the long-drawn out trial. One important fact is that those who were punished belonged to the ranks of constable, head constable and sub-inspectors/SHOs, but no one from higher ranks. The trial court had observed that in a case where ten men were slain with impunity, there was no possibility that senior functionaries of the police were not actively in the picture and criticised the CBI for not having been able to bring them to justice.

The convicted policemen went in appeal to the Allahabad High Court. The bench of Justice Ramesh Sinha and Justice Saroj Yadav held on 15 December 2022, that there was no animosity between the police personnel and those who were killed and that the appellants were public servants who acted with the advancement of public justice as their goal. The court acknowledged that the appellants exceeded the scope of their legal authority and thus, exposed themselves to the rigours of the legal system. The High Court concluded that the appellants' conviction and sentence under Sections 302 (murder), 364, 365 (kidnapping), 218 (public servant framing incorrect record), 117 (abetting commission of offence) and 120-B (criminal conspiracy) of the IPC, awarded by the trial court, was not justified. Instead, it held them guilty under Section 304 Part I (homicide not amounting to murder coupled with the element of intention to kill) of the IPC, and awarded a sentence of rigorous imprisonment of seven years and a fine of Rs 10,000 each.

One of the victims, when asked to comment on the verdict of the High Court said, "We are the ones who are suffering a never-ending punishment, not the accused policemen." She added that survivors like her are "still hurting from the memories of not having been able to see their husbands' and sons' dead bodies."

The victims have had to go once again for legal remedy to heal their lifelong wounds. The over three-decades-old judicial process has now reached the top court of the country. The Supreme Court has been approached through a special leave petition to evaluate the verdict of the Allahabad High Court of reducing the seriousness of the offence and bringing down the quantum of punishment awarded by the trial court. This has to be understood in the context of the CBI prosecutor's request for capital punishment to the accused. Even the CBI Special Court's decision for life imprisonment was not actually one that ameliorated the victims' immeasurable hurt, but the watered-down punishment from the High Court has only multiplied their woes.

* * *

Are police 'encounters' true to their dictionary meaning? Let us look at the definition most commonly found in the numerous lexicons — 'unexpectedly be faced with or experience (something hostile or difficult)'. Clearly, the element of something happening unexpectedly, which in the context of a law enforcement body dealing with hostile law-breakers would indicate that there were circumstances which precipitated out of the blue and the only option left was to use force in self-defence and that the opponents were threatening the safety of life and limb, is rare. The law defines this concept as the 'right of private defence'. There should never be a problem with such a provision. Unless law-keepers enjoy the fortification of law to use justifiable force in dealing with violent criminals, there would be a threat of the forces feeling enfeebled and the perpetrators gaining an upper hand. The society will be exposed to grave danger if the writ of the government's law-keeping machinery is not adequately vigorous to repulse the might of criminals.

The trouble starts when the extent of liberty that is permitted by the state to the armed forces, in what can be described as a '*laissez-faire* policy', spills out of control and force is used in a trigger-happy manner. This undesirable meaning of the term 'encounter' has unfortunately become the most widely accepted interpretation. Much worse is a situation where the chief minister is perceived to be in favour of eliminating selected 'criminals' in staged violence. This is seen to be a shortcut to gain brownie points. Officers who indulge in such unethical killings are often feted for their 'gallantry'. In Uttar Pradesh, there was a provision under which an out-of-turn promotion was also permissible in cases where an encounter was carried out by an official. Later this was withdrawn owing to the criticism it rightly deserved from activists and law courts.

I recall that during the tenure of V. P. Singh as UP's CM, he had shown appreciation for the elimination of criminals through encounters. A minister who worked in his government, Rajendra Tripathi, was in charge of the police department. I remember having attended a meeting sometime in 1980 in Orai, district Jalaun, in which this minister had come with a list of criminals that he had shortlisted for being eliminated. In the presence of the state's police chief, he told us that failure to account for these desperados would invite his and the CM's displeasure. With this diktat, when the officers went back to their jurisdictions, they carried two clear impressions—firstly, there was an expectation that the police would become trigger-happy and secondly, they could do this with impunity because the political leadership had granted approval for this practice. It was no surprise, therefore, that there were many encounter killings all over the state and the government claimed success in controlling crime.

This model of identifying criminals with the idea to eliminate them in encounters was followed more recently in UP once again and it seemed that this had earned the approval of the people, because the government returned with a handsome majority for a second term in the most populous state of the country.

There was a widely discussed case of the encounter killing of four alleged rapists in Hyderabad. In fact, it was a brutal killing in the early hours of 6 December 2019, which had been described, not surprisingly, as a work of justice by the Telangana police. A story was handed out claiming that while the four suspects were being taken to the scene of the gang rape they were accused of being involved in, they snatched weapons from the policemen with the intention to kill them. It was, therefore, claimed that it was an act of private defence which is justified in law. There was hue and cry from human rights groups, but they were apparently far outnumbered by those who thought that the killing of the four alleged perpetrators was the best way to deal with rapists. These people heaped praise on all the ten policemen who had taken part in the encounter.

However, the Supreme Court set up a commission under Justice V. S. Sirpurkar to probe the matter that was claimed by the police to be an act of private defence in the face of a threat to their lives. In its report submitted to the apex court in a sealed cover, the Commission found the police version to be false and said that it believed that the police had deliberately fired on the accused 'with an intent to cause their death'. The Commission recommended action against ten police officers and personnel under various charges, including murder, common intent, causing disappearance of evidence and providing false information.

On 21 May 2022, the Supreme Court ordered that the report submitted in a sealed cover by the Sirpurkar Commission be shared and transferred the matter to the Telangana High Court for subsequent action. The report stated that those who had been killed were most likely incorrectly identified as the perpetrators. Two of those who met their end were, in fact, not even adults.[19]

This is one of the many cases in which the courts have been constrained to order action against erring trigger-happy policemen. The National Human Rights Commission (NHRC) has also been active in identifying fake encounter cases and has, over the years, initiated action against a large number of policemen. Between the years 2000 and 2017, the NHRC registered 1,782 fake encounter cases. Earlier, between 1993 and 2009, at least 2,560 cases of encounters were examined by the NHRC out of which 1,224 were found to be fake. Such high numbers have been reported in spite of the fact that there is gross under-reporting of such cases in police records. The relatives of victims also prefer to maintain silence because they fear being targeted for retribution.

Many of these staged encounters receive wide media coverage and are spoken of in glowing terms. The 'other' side of the picture is obliterated and often not debated. However, when the fake aspects of the action by the police are brought up, the discourse comes to a point where all accusing fingers point in only one direction – the perpetrating policemen. The men in khaki are easily identified as participants in the bloody overreach of their duties. What lies behind their misdemeanour is equally important and must not be ignored. Experts on police matters point out these aspects as well. For instance, Prakash Singh, one of the best known police officers of the country and an acknowledged authority on matters of

19 https://www.deccanchronicle.com/nation/crime/200522/sc-sends-hyderabad-encounter-probe-report-to-hc-orders-its-sharing-wi.html

police reforms, says that the police resort to extrajudicial killings owing to the pressure from political quarters. He underlines that it is important to 'understand the whole political ecosystem, wherein the police have not only lost their independence, but also their autonomy'.[20]

One of the time-honoured principles of the Indian criminal justice system is the acknowledgement in law, supported by repeated judicial pronouncements, that the investigation of a crime is the responsibility of the police and interference in this activity from any quarters is strongly disapproved. Yet, the practice on the ground is often not in keeping with this principle. This is to what Mr Singh is drawing attention. He elaborates, "Whenever a major crime of any kind takes place, a politician steps in and tells the police officer in charge to solve the case within twenty-four hours. In such cases, the police are caught in a bind. I've seen this happen a lot of times."

However, it is not merely the politicians who encourage policemen to employ extrajudicial methods; the public at large in India has the tendency to applaud what they consider 'instant justice'. This happened in the Hyderabad encounter as well. The public supported the killing of the four suspects because they thought that the unduly long judicial process was a hindrance in delivering due punishment to the wrongdoers. We have often heard the public opinion strongly advocating such shortcuts as the idea of justice. There are any number of instances where

---

20 Quoted in the *Outlook* magazine, dated 15 August 2022. https://www.outlookindia.com/national/fake-encounters-in-india-laws-flaws-fear-magazine-213923

fake encounter killings have been celebrated and the policemen who staged them, wildly cheered. To illustrate this point, let us consider what Jaya Bachchan, an MP and much-admired actor, had to say about the Hyderabad case when the news of the rape of the vet had come, "I don't know how many times I have stood and spoken about this kind of '*atyachar*'. I think it is time, whether it is Nirbhaya, Kathua or what happened in Hyderabad, that people want the government to give a proper answer and a very definite answer." She further said, "I know it is harsh but these people should be brought out in public and lynched." When the encounter took place, her comment was, "*Der aaye, durust aaye...der aaye, bohot der aaye*... (They did the right thing, albeit with much delay)".

Article 21 of the Constitution says that 'no person shall be deprived of his life or personal liberty except according to procedure established by law'. India is also a party to the International Covenant on Civil and Political Rights, whose Article 6 states that 'every human being has the inherent right to life and this right shall be protected by law'.

It is, however, the process of law which is often cited as the reason for the approval of such heinous transgressions of human rights and wanton disregard of the law. This tellingly highlights the need to fix our judicial procedures starting from the police station, through all levels of courts, going right up to the Legislature. We need to bring urgency into the reform initiatives that are long overdue in the whole chain of the delivery of criminal justice.

The Indian police came face to face with militancy in different stages. The north-east had the first experience, followed by Kashmir and Punjab. Uttar Pradesh had its first brush with militancy in the early part of the 1990s. The state police, despite its long record of services to the state and the nation, faced an altogether different poser in the sudden onset of militancy, one for which they were not trained and even less prepared.[21] It has to be said that the response at the level of the police and the government (bureaucracy) was of novice standard, while, as often happens, the political leadership went into denial mode. It is possible to state the order of things in the reverse as well, with full justification. The government was in denial, leading to a negative response from the bureaucracy to whatever the police had to report from the ground and deny any upgradation of resources. Specially trained men, suitable weapons to match what the adversary had in its arsenal as well as experienced leadership that was adept at strategizing and leading the charge, were all a distant dream for the police on the ground. The response was knee-jerk, unplanned and quite frankly, puerile.

The SHOs were left to their own devices, the supervising officers were fumbling too and the intelligence machinery was largely clueless. Even the obvious was being swept under the carpet at whatever level there was a need to stand up and state the facts as they were, a prerequisite for any plan of action to address the problem facing us. It was, in a way, not a surprise that Inspector-General A. P. Mishra sent a report to the government, under what appears to be undue pressure, to whitewash signature militant-style attacks and other acts, to say that it was the officers at the district-level, namely, District Magistrate Sharda Prasad

21 The unexpected appearance of militants in certain pockets of UP, notably the Terai districts was the result of definitive action against militancy in Punjab.

and I, who had panicked and created noise, which had its roots in our 'inefficiency' and 'lack of experience'. He did this despite his earlier assertion made in public domain – 'The recent cases were aimed to create terror. These were not just survival crimes which the terrorists have been committing in the past in this region.'[22]

The consequences of this report were the orders handing out new postings to both Sharda Prasad and I. My successor must have been chosen on the basis of his past record of dealing with 'criminals' in, to put it mildly, a conclusive manner. There were several instances related to his earlier assignments in which his role had been under the scanner for use of excessive force leading to the killing of alleged offenders.[23]

The trigger-happy leadership style at the helm of the district can be identified as the reason why all forty-seven policemen were convicted. This matter brings into sharp focus the other side of the picture – that of perpetrators not being punished, even when there are strong reasons to conclude that they had played a role in the episode. Apart from those who were punished by the CBI court in this case, there was sufficient reason to believe that all the three district-level supervising officers were also present at

---

22 Terrorism's new threat - India Today https://www.indiatoday.in/magazine/special-report/story/19900531-punjab-terrorists-establish-terai-as-their-new-base-812651-1990-05-30

23 Incidentally, my predecessor, S. P. Srivastava, had brought the facts to the knowledge of all the important decision makers. He had also developed a good information network and was responsible for taking a few well thought-out steps to deal with the situation. Had he continued, as indeed he should have, then possibly the fake encounters that were resorted to subsequently might have been avoided.

the locations where the carnage took place.[24] They were, however, not included in the CBI charge sheet on the grounds that on the date of the occurrence, they were on leave of duty. It appears highly unlikely that on the same date, three senior officers in the chain of command dealing with the militants were expendable; yet it was found acceptable by the CBI and none of these officers were punished.

I feel that such largesse of the criminal justice system is a contributing factor leading to a sense of impunity that the police often enjoy when there are allegations of extrajudicial acts. The verdict passed by the apex court in the Hyderabad encounter will have to be counted as an exception rather than the norm. In more cases than not, the police records manage to present a picture which provides that one loophole in the story which proves enough to allow an escape route. If the judicial scrutiny in courts was more

---

24 'The court observed that the decision of dividing the victims into three groups, killing them in three different police station areas of Pilibhit and making the incident look like an encounter could not be taken solely by the convicts. It said that police officers who were holding important posts must be behind the incident, but the CBI kept them away from the investigation.'
'The court also observed that the investigating officer of the CBI was not fully free and had to regularly take directions and advice from his senior officers. While acting on their directions, several persons, who should have been accused, were set free by the investigating officers. In this case also, important persons who were part of the conspiracy could not be made accused, it said.'
1991 Pilibhit fake encounter: CBI court awards life sentence to 47 cops | India News, The Indian Express https://indianexpress.com/article/india/india-news-india/pilibhit-fake-encounter-all-47-convicted-policemen-sentenced-to-life-imprisonment/

exacting, then the licence that reckless policemen seem to take for granted would be a thing of the past.

The dreadful reality is that the encounter culture continues to be feted by the public at large. The continued popularity of the government in a few states accrues much from its record of bringing in what may be labelled as the 'encounter raj'. The official figures and reports in reliable media organizations tell us that in Uttar Pradesh alone, between March 2017 and April 2022, there were 9,434 encounters, 139 'criminals' were killed between March 2017 and June 2021 and 3,196 'criminals' were injured. The injured included those who were targets of what is unofficially called 'operation *langda*' wherein the bullet injury is inflicted on the leg leading to disability. In other words, what was detestable and a gross violation of human rights in the 20th century continues to be much in practice in the 21st century, supported by the fawning admiration of the society.

The moot question that is thrown up by this fact is that does the public want the rule of law to be replaced by extrajudicial methods? Are the human rights groups of any consequence in a society where pain inflicted on others finds no empathy in fellow human beings? Will this disabling of the social framework ever be reformed sufficiently to accommodate the true rule of law? Will the bleak colonial system that we continue to have make way for a just and expeditious modern process which is known not for its sloth and inefficiency, but for its vigour and devotion to deliver justice?

Students of the social sciences tell us that the trigger-happy police have never been successful in bringing down crime. In fact, when those targeted are victims of police excesses and not the actual perpetrators of crime, the real culprits gain a fresh lease to continue their depredations. If you add this to our ineffective judicial machinery and the inaccessibility of legal recourse to millions of victims of crime, you will end up with a dreary outlook which will make you very sad.

In an encounter, no charges are communicated to the alleged criminal, no opportunity is provided for defence in a court of law and the provision of representation by a lawyer is, of course, not even in the picture. The Supreme Court has interpreted significant facets as being a part of the right to life under Article 21.[25] These include the right to a speedy and fair trial and the right to free legal aid from the state if the accused cannot afford representation. Clearly, the Constitution has evaluated the life of each individual as precious and considers it incumbent upon the state to establish a system of criminal justice which assures each person due process of law, including a fair trial leading to suitable punishment for the committed offence. In more cases than not, the prosecution fails to establish the accused person's guilt to exacting standards, especially when the charges are of the commitment of heinous offences. The statistics of the government show that the conviction of the accused persons in heinous offences is single-digit number per cent. For this reason, it is even more telling that merely on the basis of suspicion, someone is deprived of life, thereby awarding the maximum punishment for something which has not even been brought before a court of law for adjudication.

Let us not forget that Mohammed Ajmal Amir Kasab, a

25 https://indiankanoon.org/doc/1373215/ Supreme Court of India: Hussainara Khatoon & Ors vs Home Secretary, State Of Bihar 1979

Pakistani terrorist and a member of the Lashkar-e-Taiba Islamist terrorist organization, who was arrested in the case of the 2008 Mumbai terrorist attack, was given all opportunities to present his case before the trial court, for which, the state provided the services of an *amicus curiae*. He was also allowed to appeal in higher courts and move an application before the President for clemency. This clearly indicates that the spirit of the law is to go through the entire legal process before hanging even the deadliest of criminals, who in this case was one who participated in one of the most sensational terrorist attacks carried out on the soil of India.

All the requisite protections were also extended to the people accused of murdering Mohandas Gandhi and Indira Gandhi. In fact, it was at the Red Fort trial held after Gandhi's assassination, that Vinayak Damodar Savarkar was acquitted of all charges. Had he received the bullet of a trigger-happy policeman for the alleged crime of killing the Father of the Nation, he would not have had the opportunity to defend himself and would have been deprived of a chance to prove that there wasn't clinching evidence to sentence him along with the others who were found guilty. In the Indira Gandhi assassination case too, all the accused were provided with due opportunities to prove their innocence.

In Prakash Kadam vs. Ramprasad Vishwanath Gupta, the Supreme Court observed that fake 'encounters' by the police are nothing but cold-blooded murders and those committing them must be given death sentences, placing them in the category of the 'rarest of rare cases'. The apex court categorically stated – "We warn policemen that they will not be excused for committing murder in the name of 'encounter' on the pretext that they were carrying out the orders of their superior officers or politicians, however high. In the Nuremberg trials, the Nazi war criminals took the plea that 'orders are orders'; nevertheless, they were hanged. If a policeman is given an illegal order by any superior to carry out a fake 'encounter', it is his duty to refuse to carry out such an illegal order, otherwise he will be charged for murder and if found guilty, sentenced to death."[26]

The incarceration for life sentence awarded to the policemen who staged the 1991 carnage in Pilibhit should have served as a wake-up call for all those who employ encounters as a tool to control crime. However, has the message made the requisite difference of attitude or are the policemen still in slumber? The answer appears to be in the negative. Despite all that we have heard from the apex court and other bodies like the National Human Rights Commission, there are still a large number of decision makers who continue to not merely look the other way when fake encounters are staged by policemen, but go so far as to sing paeans in praise of these 'heroic' defenders of the law-abiding citizens. As a result, those who commit these dishonourable acts, walk away with officially recognised approval tags and medals that unabashedly label them as gallant champions.

The victims of these egregious acts are left licking their unhealable wounds. Seeking justice from the courts of law comes at a price which very few can afford. The most common denouement

---

26 https://indiankanoon.org/doc/1979158/Supreme Court: Prakash Kadam vs Ramprasad Vishwanath Gupta 13 May 2011.

of the long-drawn and intricate legal processes is, more often than not, pain heaped on an insurmountable load of grief. The entire justice system is crying out for reforms, if not an overhaul.

* * *

Postscript

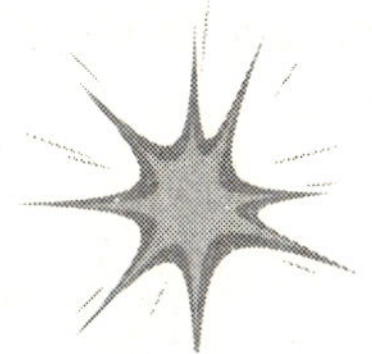

Mark Stallion, the 'general', has had an extended profile to still make appearances. I was working as IG in Uttaranchal (later renamed Uttarakhand) in the year 2001, when he was spotted in district Udham Singh Nagar. The Kashipur police station received information that he was camping in a house in village Katayya. The house was surrounded by a police party. An exchange of firing ensued. I was informed that he broke through the police cordon by firing indiscriminately at the police posse and escaped along with an accomplice. Some explosives and weapons were recovered from the scene.

In August 2019, the *panchayat* elections were underway in Uttarakhand. Once again, the police recovered a large amount of liquor in the jurisdiction of the Kashipur police station. This was an offence under law, so the persons carrying the contraband were detained. It turned out that one of the detained persons was Mark Stallion. It was revealed that he was transporting the liquor to be used by one of the candidates in the election for bribing supporters and voters. Interestingly, the officer who arrested Mark Stallion on this occasion was Chandan Singh Bisht, who was posted as my reader a decade ago.

So, the militant 'general' who was in the dusk years of his life, had graduated to being a supporter for candidates in a democratic process. I wondered if one day, he will throw his own hat into the arena to become a legislator.

Acknowledgements

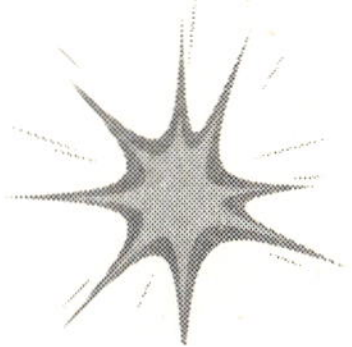

The fanning out of Khalistan militancy from Punjab into the Terai region of Uttar Pradesh posed a significant challenge to the police force of the state. However, the literature on the subject of this wave of terror that engulfed large tracts of India's most populous state is limited. We sensed an opportunity to not just inform the reader about the scenario which prevailed but also the numerous atrocities that were faced by the people of the region.

We are indebted to Suhail Mathur of 'The Books Bakers' who was instrumental in finding us a marquee publisher – Srishti. It is also in order to thank Stuti Sharma Gupta for editing the book and making it more reader-friendly.

A word of gratitude is due for Senior advocate of the Supreme Court R. S. Sodhi and advocate Harjinder Singh Kahlon who were generous in providing us authentic material about the ongoing legal battle. We appreciate the Superintendent of Police, Pilibhit, Atul Sharma IPS, for being forthcoming with important bits from the police records.

To our family and friends, we are beholden.